MW00439122

Travel Happy, Budget Low

Over 200 Money Saving Tips to See the World

Enrich yourself culturally without being rich!

Susanna Zaraysky

Dedication

To my loving parents Isak and Rimma Zaraysky. Even though you might have regretted my wanderlust, especially when I chose to go to bizarre places most people couldn't spell or find on the map, I am deeply grateful that you taught my sister Asya and I to love to travel.

To my self-destructive and flying passports. You not only accompanied me during my tragic-comic airport fiascos, you have also caused many a folly in my travels. Let's see what my new passport has in store for me!

To whatever soul created the idea of frequent flyer miles. Thank you!

Advance Praise for *Travel Happy, Budget Low*

"Susanna has written a digestible, yet comprehensive, guide to help travelers save money, be comfortable, journey light and stay happy in the process!"

-Beth Whitman, author of the Wanderlust and Lipstick guides for women travelers

"Susanna is able to combine her personal experience to give the reader some essentials in seeing the world on a budget. This book will enable many folks to see more of the world for less."

-Albert Yu, Group Sales Manager, Four Seasons Silicon Valley

"A practical read and must have for any budget conscious traveler. Share in Susanna's experiences and learn from her mistakes to become a savvy globetrotter. This book is for both beginners and experienced travelers, with a wealth of tips and resources covering all areas of travel."

-Kristine Ng, Co-founder of Esplora, an online resource and social networking site for women travelers

"Ideal for those seeking an unlikely adventure; a helpful first step for someone who may consider the world far bigger and more daunting that it truly is, and a great companion for someone who wants to discover the world beyond their own backyard."

-Ian Spinks, traveled to 35 countries in four and a half years

"I found Ms. Zaraysky's book an invaluable source for an independent traveler. It is very useful, up to the point and very functional. I wish I knew some of the tips that I found in this book during my earlier travels."

-Leon Gendin, 27 years of travel, visited 63 countries, lived in 12 countries.

"Do you feel grounded by high priced airline tickets, lousy exchange rates, and luxury hotels? Susanna Zaraysky, the quintessential budget globetrotter shows you how to travel well without breaking your budget. A must read for would-be world travelers!"

-Prof. Lois Lorentzen, University of San Francisco

Travel Happy, Budget Low
Over 200 Money Saving Tips to See the World
Part of the *Create Your World* book series
Copyright © 2009 by Susanna Zaraysky.

First Edition

All rights reserved. No part of this book may be used or reproduced in any manner whatsoever without written permission from the publisher, except for brief quotations embodied in articles or reviews.

Kaleidomundi
PO Box 1253
Cupertino, CA 95015
USA
www.createyourworldbooks.com, www.kaleidomundi.com
Email: info@kaleidomundi.com

ISBN: 978-0-9820189-8-9
LCCN: 2008910799

Cover and Interior Design by Krista Anderson
Edited by Frank Reuter and Britt Breu
Photo Credits: © www.danbrady.co.uk (cover, Toutes Directions)
             © Steve Woods/sxc.hu (page 112, Money Grabber)
             http://www.sxc.hu
Typefaces used in this book are credited as follows: Futura, designed by Paul Renner; and Baskerville, designed by John Baskerville.

Create Your World Book Series

Mission

- To create global citizens who are engaged in the world, passionate about world events and confident international travelers and communicators.
- To empower you to interact and appreciate other cultures and ways of life.
- To give you the skills to travel economically and see the world.
- To teach you how to easily learn foreign languages and have fun.

Be your own peacemaker!
Be your own ambassador!
Create your world!

Books In This Series

Travel Happy, Budget Low
Over 200 Money Saving Tips to See the World

Language is Music
Over 70 Fun & Easy Tips to Learn Foreign Languages

Benefits of this book

*A traveler. By my faith, you have great reason to be sad. I
fear you have sold your own lands to see other men's. Then
to have seen much and to have nothing is to have rich eyes
and poor hands.*
ROSALIND

Yes, I have gained my experience.

JAQUES
As You Like It (Act IV, Scene 1) William Shakespeare

Unlike Shakespeare's character, I am a testament to the fact that one
can both gain experience by seeing the world and be financially sound.
This book will teach you how to do the same.

Some of the best things in life are free.

You just have to get yourself to those places or events in an economical
way. Beijing's Forbidden City and Iguazu Falls in South America took
my breath away. It doesn't cost a fortune to experience the wonders of
our planet, it just takes some planning and thinking. This book does a
lot of the work for you.

May thine eyes be rich with the world and your spirit happy on a low
travel budget!

The most costly elements of travel are transportation, lodging and
food. *Travel Happy, Budget Low* informs you how to travel economically
in planes, trains, and buses, how to find inexpensive meals, and how
to book inexpensive hotel rooms or stay for free with locals. You don't
have to look like an undergraduate hauling a backpack; in fact, I now
prefer a rolling suitcase. Over 200 tips and 161 website resources cover
the topics of frequent flyer mile tricks, health/safety, expenditures,
packing, passports/visas, preparation, customs and more.

This book is a guidebook to becoming a world traveler. Open your
horizons. Be at ease in foreign lands. Not only will you be touched by
cultures new to you, you can leave your mark on the people you visit.
May you be a responsible and courteous visitor who travels in a financially responsible way.

Table Of Contents

Section 1: Pre-trip Basics

Passports, Visas, Travel Insurance,
Discount Cards, Timing & Seasons

Plan ahead for international travel and avoid costly bureaucratic delays with passports and visas.

Passport

1. Get a Passport

While obtaining a passport may seem obvious to many, airline personnel occasionally encounter passengers checking in at the airport for an international flight without a passport. In these cases, passport-less passengers are denied entry on to the airplane and may lose the value of their ticket. If you are crossing international borders via land, a passport may not be required. Check on the website of the consulate or embassy of the country you are going to visit to verify if you need a passport.

If you are stateless–this applies mainly to refugees–an immigrant, or seeking political asylum, you will have to ask for travel papers from the Immigration Department or Ministry of the country where you reside.

In the United States, applying for a new passport through the State Department takes about four weeks and renewing a previously existing passport takes about two weeks. Some post offices handle new passport processing. It's best to check the State Department's website for information. If you apply close to the busy summer and Christmas travel seasons, you may experience delays. Expedited passport processing is expensive and requires you to visit the closest US Passport Agency on a business day. There are Passport Agencies in major US cities.

To find out how to apply for a passport or renew an old one, go **to www.state.gov**, the website for the State Department.

For an index of embassies and consulates worldwide, go to **www.embassyworld.com**

2. Before you leave your home country, check that your passport is valid for at least 90 days

Some countries will not let you enter their territory if your passport will expire within 90 or 180 days. You do not want to end up at an airport or border crossing with an almost expired passport. The border guards of a country may deny you entry, forcing you to return home at your own expense and drastically change your travel plans. Know when your passport expires.

Visas

3. Check to make sure if you need a visa for the country or countries you will be visiting

A visa is an entry permit issued by the government of the country you are visiting. There are tourist, business, educational, family reunification visas, as well as other categories of visas.

WARNING: It's your responsibility to know the visa regulations of the countries you will visit. Check with the local embassy or consulate of the country you intend to visit if you need a visa.

If you buy an incredibly cheap plane ticket that is non-changeable or refundable, you may lose your entire ticket if you arrive at the airport without a visa and are denied entry on the plane. Don't bet on the airline staff taking pity on your ignorance of visa rules and permitting you to modify a non-changeable ticket.

When you buy plane tickets on the Internet, no screen appears telling you if you do or do not need a visa. Even travel agents forget or neglect to inform clients that they require a visa for their trips. Travel guidebooks can also be out of date. Furthermore, political situations can develop quickly that cause a country to require visas from travelers from particular countries.

You should also be aware of how long you can stay in a country with your visa. There are stiff fines for overstaying visas and you may be barred from re-entering the country for many years.

Look online for the embassy or consulate of the countries you are planning on visiting and look under their visa section to see if you require a visa for you trip. Or look for the embassy or consulate in your phone book and call them. Many consulates and embassies have recorded information about visa requirements. For some countries, visas are only required for trips over 30 or 90 days. If a visa is required, you will have to fill out an application explaining the intention of your trip. Some applications ask you to indicate where you will be staying. If you haven't made a hotel reservation yet, write down an address from a hotel in your guidebook. Most likely, you will have to provide one or two passport size photos for your visa.

Find your local embassy or consulate and verify visa requirements at **www.embassyworld.com**

Personal Story

In July 2007, I went to the Brazilian Consulate in San Francisco to get my tourist visa. Two men in their 30s stood with their suitcases in the busy and hectic waiting room. They had bought their tickets to Brazil on the Internet. They arrived at the United Airlines counter at the San Francisco International Airport only to be denied entry on the plane because they didn't have a visa. (The Immigration and Customs Ministries of countries fine airlines who let passengers on board without the proper travel documents.) The two men were lucky that there was a Brazilian consulate nearby. They went to the consulate directly from the airport and applied for express visas. The consulate, however, could not promise they could process the visas within the working day. When I left the consulate a couple of hours later, the men were still waiting for their visas.

4. Obtain a visa on your own or via a visa processing company

Embassies or consulates are only open on weekdays. Furthermore, they often have limited hours for visa services. Traveling to a consulate or embassy to turn in your visa documents may require taking a day off of work, standing in a long line, or waiting in a busy waiting room. I have learned this the hard way. It may be less expensive to pay a visa processing service to handle your visa for you. All you have to do is mail them your passport, complete a visa application form that you can download from the Internet or that they mail to you, and pay the processing and mailing fees. If a visa processing company charges you $40 or $75 to take care of your visa, you should compare those prices to how much it will cost you to get to the consulate and take time off work. Some consulates won't give you a visa on the spot and you may have to return in a few days to retrieve your passport. In that case, you have to calculate how much it costs to go to the consulate or embassy twice. A visa service sends a courier to the consulates and embassies and makes sure that the visas have the correct spelling of your name and the right dates for your trip.

Make sure to give yourself enough time to get the visas. Embassies and consulates honor the national holidays of the countries where they are located and their own national ones. This means they have more holidays then you probably do.

Most embassies and consulates do not accept personal checks. They only take money orders or cashiers checks. Some may accept credit cards. Check with the consulate for instructions. If you want them to mail your passport and visa back to you, follow their mailing instructions carefully. If they say to bring a post office return envelope or a FedEx one, don't come with a UPS one. They may not accept it.

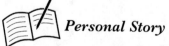 *Personal Story*

I had to rush to get my Chinese visa in February 2008 because the

Chinese consulate was closed for a few days during Chinese New Year. I wanted to save myself the trip to San Francisco to pick up my visa and asked a friend to get it for me. When my friend got home from the consulate and opened my passport, he called me and told me that the Chinese had re-baptized me and given me a new surname. I had to take a day off work and go up to San Francisco to fix the mistake and get a new visa.

Check for the procedures for your visa application: **www.embassyworld.com**

Visa processing companies in the US: **www.travisa.com**

www.traveldocs.com

5. The disadvantages/advantages of getting a visa when you're abroad

If you are on a multi-country trip and will first go to a country where you don't need a visa or you already have a visa for the first country or countries of your trip, then you might consider getting visas for the other countries on your itinerary that require them before you leave home. Or you can acquire them when you are already abroad. I have done the latter on several occasions but do not recommend it most of the time. When you are abroad, you want to spend your time seeing the sights and not standing in line in a consulate or worrying that the travel agent who promised that his brother has a "speedy visa" service will return with your passport and visa promptly. Quick visa service abroad may be expensive. Check your guidebook for information on visa services in specific countries or on Lonely Planet's Thorn Tree forum where travelers share their stories. If other travelers say it's simple and fast to get the visa in a neighboring country, then consider doing it there.

The only advantage to getting the visa abroad is when you are going to a country that does not have a consulate near where you live and does not accept visa applications by mail.

www.lonelyplanet.com/thorntree

Personal Story

In 2007, I was in Thailand on my way to Cambodia and Vietnam. A French traveler, who had already done the same trip from Thailand to Siem Riep, Cambodia, told me not to overpay for my Cambodian visa through the travel agency arranging the mini bus to Cambodia and suggested I just buy the visa at the border. His advice sounded good.

I was in for a surprise.

About 12 of us foreigners were crammed into a mini bus to the Cambodian border. We stopped in a restaurant for a break and met with a big busload of tourists who were traveling from Bangkok, Thailand to Siem Riep, Cambodia. The travel agency took everyone into a room and asked us to fill out Cambodian visa documents if we didn't already have a visa. They were charging an extra $30 "processing fee" for the visas. Two Norwegian fellows and a tall German man agreed with me to get the visa at the Thai-Cambodian border and not pay the travel agency's bogus fee. Of course, the Thai bus company tried to convince us that we could not buy visas at the border, but we didn't want to succumb to their rip off games. When we got to the border, the tour company representative made the Norwegians, the German, and I go to the front of the line to pass through Thai customs. Most of the *rest of the people on the minibus stayed behind. After we went through the Thai side, we had to go to the Cambodian visa office to apply for visas. The travel agency person said something to the Cambodian visa clerks. As soon as we came to pick up the visa applications, the Cambodian visa officer told us the visas were $20 more expensive than the price listed on the sign above his window.*

"That's an old sign," the clerk told me when I asked why I had to pay more than the listed price.

He was just asking us for more money because the travel agency representative told him to do so. The travel agency's revenge didn't stop there.

The Cambodian colleagues of the Thai travel agents told the German guy, the two Norwegians, and me that our bus to Siem Riep had broken down. Instead of an air conditioned bus, we bumped up and down for five hours on a dusty unpaved road in a pick-up truck. Almost everyone else on the mini-bus who had paid the $30 fee or had previously obtained their visa in Bangkok got to ride on a normal bus to Siem Riep after we left in the pick-up truck.

If I had processed my Cambodian visa back at home, I could have avoided the bribery and the extremely dusty and bumpy pick-up truck ride from hell.

6. Visa Photos

In case you need to get a visa abroad, bring some extra color passport-size photos of yourself that you can use for visas. This will save you time in looking for a photo service company while traveling.

7. Travel insurance

I've lost money on trips when I didn't have insurance. I had to pay for medical services myself. I've seen others make the same mistake and have to pay for the entire cost of a vacation they never took because of circumstances forcing them to cancel their trip. Trip cancellation insurance would reimburse your costs in cases of justified medical necessity. Buy travel insurance for medical emergencies, trip cancellation and theft. Make sure that your travel insurance company has trained nursing staff and claims' representatives available 24 hours a day and seven days a week, including holidays. Ask if the insurance company has offices or contact phone numbers in the areas you are visiting.

Enter the dates of your trip, and the website will show you a comparison chart of the fees of various travel insurance companies at: **www.insuremytrip.com**

 Personal Story:

Although I have never personally had to file a travel insurance claim, in March 2008, I was traveling in a group in Taiwan when one of the group members fell of a cliff and broke his leg. I had to call International Medical Group, our travel insurance company, to file the claim and ask for permission for certain hospital charges. The company was only open during the regular business hours of the Central Time Zone in the United States and had no office in Taiwan. There was a 13 hour time difference between Taiwan and the agency's offices in the United States. I could only reach the insurance company if I called after 11pm or so, which I did after sitting a 12-hour shift at the hospital with my teammate. I was exhausted and extremely annoyed with the travel insurance company. They had no nurses on staff during non-business hours who had the authority to approve medical charges

and procedures. I had to leave messages with an answering service that did not know where Taiwan was, couldn't spell, and accidentally dropped my calls. I was furious. Choose your insurers wisely.

8. International Student Identity Card (ISIC), International Youth Travel Card (IYTC) or International Teacher Identity Card (ITIC)

This card is the Cadillac of the budget traveler. It's a must!

If you are going to travel aboard, identity cards are a real value. I wish I could still qualify for an ISIC and get all the discounts and advantages of the card. In order to be eligible for an ISIC, you must be a student aged 12 & over currently enrolled at an accredited institution and matriculating towards a diploma or a degree. Continuing education and language school students are not eligible. With the card, you can get discount student airfares, access to over 33,000 discounts in over 100 countries, international recognition of your full-time student status, 24-hour Help Line emergency service, and basic sickness and accident travel insurance (for trips outside the US). Do yourself a favor and buy the $22 card. The card's benefits far outweigh its small cost. People under the age of 26 and full time teachers and faculty can also qualify for similar discount cards.

You can buy the card at your local STA travel agency, **www.statravel.com** or **www.myisic.com**

Personal Story

When I studied in Argentina in 1999 as a Rotary Ambassadorial Scholar, I forgot to get a new card for the following year and truly regretted not buying it. In January 2000, I was traveling with my sister in neighboring Brazil. I sprained my ankle on the cobblestone stairs of colonial Ouro Preto. My trip to Brazil was ruined. I had to return to the US immediately and had to pay for a last minute ticket to Buenos Aires to pick up my belongings. If I had the travel insurance from the ISIC, some of my travel costs for my trip back to Argentina on my way home to California would have been covered.

9. 'Tis the Season *not* to travel

The flights to London in February are cheap and you think it's time for you to see Big Ben. Bring a parka. Plane fares are inexpensive during certain times of the year for a reason. It's either cold, hot, rainy, foggy, or a just plain miserable time to visit. You want to see the Taj Mahal? Make sure it's not monsoon season in India. When it's cold where you are, think of going to the opposite hemisphere for sunlight. Check weather conditions on the Weather Channel online, in your newspaper or look at a guidebook for general climatic patterns for the area you want to see. Guidebooks indicate the best times of year to visit.

www.weather.com

10. Festivals

If you hate alcohol and seeing crowds of drunk people acting silly, avoid Munich's yearly Octoberfest beer festival. However, if you and beer are inseparable, plan your German vacation to coincide with the yearly revelry. Flights to East Asia can be very expensive in January and February because of the Lunar New Year. Guidebooks usually list a yearly calendar of festivals. When traveling to a city during a major sporting event like the French Open, you may not be able to find inexpensive accommodations unless you book well in advance. Plan ahead!

11. Free travel seminars and talks

Large outdoor outfitters such as REI and small local outdoor gear suppliers frequently offer free travel seminars on a variety of topics throughout the year. Contact your local branch or store to inquire about their offerings.

Both national chain and independent bookstores are also a good resource for free travel talks. Many bookstores will host travel authors promoting their new books. Check your bookstore's website for more information.

www.rei.com

Section 2: Packing

Gadgets, Electronics, Packing
Techniques, Luggage, Guidebooks,
Maps, How To Hide Your Money

Gadgets & Electronics

12. Earplugs and Noise Cancellation Headphones

The bus driver of your 24-hour bus trip is blasting local folk music on the radio and everyone on the bus is singing along—except you because the noise is giving you a migraine. Loud planes, trains, buses, ferries, and hotels can make traveling and sleeping difficult. Your economic accommodations may happen to be near a busy street or bus stop. Earplugs are cheap and can help you sleep by tuning out noise. They are almost indispensable when you are sitting on a plane, train, or bus next to crying babies or loud passengers whose conversations or music you don't want to hear.

Noise cancellation headphones hush ambient noise by creating antinoise that decrease the noise at your ear. Unfortunately, they don't completely eliminate noise, but the better models significantly reduce the whoosh of airplanes' air-conditioning systems. Noise-canceling headphones come in all forms, from full size to earbuds. The Bose headphones are the most popular, but they also cost around $300.

13. Adapters and Convertors

In the United States, our electric devices work on a 110-volt current. Other countries use 220-volt currents and may have different looking plugs. You will need to buy convertors and adaptor plugs to use in different countries. If your electric devices do not already come with an converter that will switch from the 110 volt current to the 220 volt current, then buy one. Most blow dryers and laptop computers are sold with a built-in converter. The Travel Smart adapter/convertor from Conair (previously under the Franzus brand) has five polarized adapter plugs, a surge protector and a transformer from 220V to 110V electricity. If you are visiting a tourist area like Hong Kong, these products are easily available and inexpensive.

See next page for website resources.

www.kropla.com is a website with plug and voltage information by country, including pictures of the plugs and electric outlets. You can also find the products you need to buy for your electronics.

www.franzus.com or www.conair.com/travel-accessories-c-55.html is the website for the Travel Smart Adaptor/Converter.

14. Immersion Heater

Do you need your tea or coffee in the morning? Do you need a hot drink before going to bed? A simple immersion heater is an appliance that will save you money daily. An immersion heater is an electric coil used to boil water. People on a limited budget who are avoiding restaurant meals find it invaluable. Place it in a cup of water, plug it in, and you will quickly have boiling water. (Don't use a plastic cup as it may melt. You can use a metallic cup but you should be careful when touching it as it may be hot.) It not only kills all disease-causing organisms, it also lets you make a hot cup of tea, coffee, cocoa, or soup. You can even cook an egg by bringing the water to a boil, removing the heater, dropping in the egg, and waiting a few minutes.

Small, lightweight immersion heaters are inexpensive and available in dual voltages, though you may still need a plug adapter. You can buy a new immersion heater locally in most developed countries. Better-quality versions of these have thermostatic shut-offs. If you purchase a cheaper one, be sure that the coil is immersed in liquid whenever the unit is plugged in.

www.letravelstore.com Check here for immersion heaters and other travel products.

15. Rechargeable batteries and charger

If your camera, CD player, and other portable electronic items require batteries, consider buying rechargeable batteries and a charger. You will save money this way instead of constantly buying batteries for your appliances. It's also better for the environment to use rechargeable batteries than buying disposable ones. Make sure the charger has an adapter, or buy one if you are traveling to a country with a different voltage system.

16. Extra memory card
Camera memory cards can be very expensive abroad, especially in touristy areas. If you want to download your photos to your computer and want to have a backup in case your computer gets stolen while abroad, bring an extra memory card. Most electronics are more expensive abroad than in the US, so do your shopping at home.

17. Flashlight
It's wise to have a small, battery powered flashlight. If you stay in a hostel with dormitory style rooms, you and your dorm mates will appreciate your flashlight. When you enter the room late at night and everyone else is sleeping, you can use your flashlight to rummage through your backpack to find your toothbrush instead of turning on the lights and waking everyone up.

18. Reverse the batteries
To prevent your battery powered objects from turning on by themselves while shifting around in your bags, reverse the battery position by putting the plus or minus signs of the batteries in the opposite direction so they won't auto activate. You can also take out the batteries and place them in a separate bag or container when you are not using the battery powered objects.

19. Battery powered alarm clock
A small battery operated alarm clock is indispensable. You may need to wake up early to get to the train station; not all hostels or other inexpensive accommodations like bungalows have wake up call service.

Luggage & Packing

20. Rolling backpack suitcases with big wheels

I've recently discovered the ease and comfort of traveling with a small suitcase with big wheels that also converts into a backpack. Samsonite, Swiss Gear, and other manufacturers make these convertible suitcases with a special padded pouch for laptop computers. This feature is wonderful because it's easy to take the laptop in and out of the suitcase, and I don't have to bother wrapping it in a sweater or something thick to protect it from hitting other items in my suitcase. The big wheels make it easy to roll the suitcase around. Small wheels break and chip easily, thus making it hard to roll the suitcase around. More expensive models have 360 degree wheels. When I have to walk up stairs and I don't want to carry the suitcase in one hand, I just unwrap the backside of the suitcase, take out the backpack straps, and clip them to the bottom of the suitcase. Versatility and practicality make traveling much easier.

www.samsonite.com

21. Colored suitcases or marked suitcases

Make your luggage stand out for easy recognition. Black suitcases are the most common. Although my purple suitcase makes people laugh, I can spot it easily on a luggage carousel while everyone else is squinting at all the black and gray suitcases to see which one of them is theirs. If you do have a common looking piece of luggage, put a big piece of tape on it with your initials or wrap colored rope around it so that you can easily spot it. Don't tie ribbons or scarves on the suitcase handles as they might get stuck in the carousel.

22. Carry-on bags

I love to travel without checking in my luggage, but when I go for long trips or am carrying liquid containers that are larger than

3oz or 100ml, I have to check in my bags. Traveling with only carry-on bags makes sense because you can leave the airport more quickly after landing and going through customs (for international flights). You don't have to wait at baggage carousels or worry about your lost bags. (London's Heathrow Airport is notorious for losing luggage.) If you do opt to fly with just carry-ons, then make sure your luggage is small enough to fit into the overhead compartments on the plane. Check airline websites for acceptable carry-on bag sizes. Take all of your valuables like cameras, jewelry, computer equipment on board with you. Luggage may get lost and baggage handlers can steal items from suitcases. Check airline websites for acceptable carry-on bag sizes.

23. Small containers of liquids in carry-on baggage

Liquids, gels and/or aerosols are permitted through security checkpoints. Items must fit in one clear, re-sealable quart or liter-sized plastic bag, in containers of 3oz/100ml or less. Many countries have the same standards as the US.

www.tsa.gov/travelers This is the Transportation Safety Agency's website with informational for travelers flying to and from the US.

24. Clothing and toiletries for one day

If you separate your items between carry-on bags and checked-in luggage, make sure to pack enough clothes and toiletries for at least one day. Your checked suitcase may be delayed and you will want to change your clothes, brush your teeth and handle other hygiene matters after your flight. Make sure your liquid items don't exceed the maximum allowed quantity as described above.

25. Locks

If you are traveling in the US and you want to lock your suitcase or bag to prevent theft, make sure to get locks that are approved by the US Transportation Safety Administration (TSA). Since the TSA may need to open your bags for inspection, they only allow a certain type of lock which they can open with a master key.

www.safeskieslocks.com
www.travelsentry.org

26. Vacuum packing bags (Travel Space Bags)

My recent discovery of vacuum packing bags has been wonderful. The plastic bags come in different sizes, each of which will carry several pieces of clothing. By simply squeezing and rolling, you can remove the air that creates bulk. Just fill the bag with your clothes, roll it to push out the air, seal it, and pack it in your luggage. You can reduce the volume in your luggage by 50% with these bags. They are great for bulky items like sweaters and pillows. If you have wet garments or dirty laundry, you can pack them in these bags and you won't have to worry about the smell or moisture of the clothes stinking up your entire suitcase or bag. In the United States, these bags are available at The Container Store, Home Depot, Target, and online retailers such as Amazon.

www.spacebag.com/travelbag

27. Extra plastic or cloth bags

Always pack some extra compact bags that you can use for dirty laundry, packing or even when shopping. In some countries, you get charged for each plastic bag you use at a grocery store. Save a few cents and create less trash.

28. Travel pouch

This is probably the most important item to bring with you besides your wallet. Pickpockets love to lurk in your pockets, bags, backpacks, purses, and wallets. You need to hide your passport, money, plane tickets, credit and bank cards from them. Travel pouches are like cloth envelopes with one or two pockets in which you can store your valuables. You can buy these in most travel and luggage supply stores or online. Some travel pouches hang from your neck. I advise against these as thieves can cut the band around your neck and catch the falling travel pouch. The safest pouch is a cloth travel belt with an elastic band worn around your waist. It can be very inconvenient to wear, especially when it is hot and you don't want a big bulge on your stomach that makes you look weird. Put only crucial items in the pouch and avoid carrying physically large amounts of cash. I suggest putting the pouch on the bottom of your back between your pants and undergarments. You should keep your passport in a plastic re-sealable bag.

 ### *Personal story*

While traveling in Kiev in 1997, I had a travel pouch on my stomach. It was raining outside. The moisture on my skin seeped through the travel pouch and got the gold eagle paint on the outside of my passport wet. The gold paint went through the material of my passport and stained my passport photo, making it look fake. This was a disaster as I was leaving later the same day and had to go through customs with a suspicious looking passport. Lesson learned. I now keep my passport in a re-sealable (Ziploc) bag inside my travel pouch.

www.eaglecreek.com
www.worldtraveler.com

29. Hidden money belt

To really hide your money, you can fold your bills and stuff them into a hidden zippered security pocket within a belt that safely conceals currency. You wear the belt like a normal belt around your pants. It's adjustable and comes in just one size. This is a good option if you are afraid of getting something stolen. You can't put your passport or credit cards into this belt because it's too narrow, but it is a good place to hide money. Unless someone robs you and makes you strip your clothes, you should be safe.

www.eaglecreek.com

30. Pack light!

With airlines charging for checked luggage to cover the cost of rising fuel costs, it's more important than ever to travel light. The truth is that you won't need most of the clothes and items that you think you need. The lighter your luggage, the easier it is for you to move around. Many subway systems don't have escalators and you will have to haul your luggage by hand. Older hotels also may not have elevators. Be prepared to carry whatever you pack, as well as whatever you buy while traveling. If you can barely lift your suitcases at home, start over and remove half of your belongings, making sure you are taking just the bare minimum.

31. Clothing optional...

It's wise for women to bring a long sleeved shirt and long skirt or pants in case you enter a place of worship. Some places won't admit you in a short sleeved shirt, shorts or short skirt. A head scarf may be needed if entering a mosque or Eastern Orthodox Church. Men also should not enter a mosque in shorts and a tank top. Be respectful of holy sites and dress accordingly.

Forget carrying all your nice clothes with you. If you will mostly be walking in cities and you might go to a concert or theater, then pack one nice outfit or make sure you have a presentable pair of pants, shirt, blouse, or skirt that you could wear in a formal setting. Women can dress up a plain shirt with a scarf or vest. Be creative and think light. If you think that you may not pack enough clothes to last you for a week of traveling, remember that you can always wash your clothes in your hotel/hostel rooms.

32. Books
Long distance travel affords you a lot of time to read. However, carrying lots of reading material will weigh down your suitcase. Many hostels and budget hotels have book exchange shelves where travelers can leave their books and pick up new ones. Southeast Asia has many used bookstores carrying books in most Western European languages. Books are heavy, so don't overload on reading materials!

33. Travel pillows
Long flights, train and bus rides can make our necks feel horrible. An inflatable neck pillow wraps around your neck and prevents neck strain. It provides a comfortable cushion for your neck when you fall asleep. The pillow is easy to carry. It's a foldable pouch that you blow air into and then deflate when you are done.

www.ezysleep.com
www.eaglecreek.com/accessories/
travel_comfort/

34. Slippers
It's always good to have your own pair of slippers. After a day of walking, you will want to take off your shoes and rest in your hotel room with slippers. You can use the slippers for the beach or pool areas as well. Most Asian hotels provide slippers.

35. Comfortable walking shoes
This point is very important. Pack at least two pairs of comfortable shoes. Sneakers may not be appropriate if you go to a nice restaurant, the theater, or a concert. Make sure to have at least one pair of comfortable shoes that look decent. In case it rains or you step in mud, you will want a second pair of shoes as a spare.

You may be traveling in places with unpaved streets, cobblestone roads, or lunar surfaced streets with many holes. I always laugh at the women walking in stiletto heals on old streets. They are accidents waiting to happen.

36. Hanging toiletries bag with a hanger
The most convenient toiletries bags for all your personal hygiene, cosmetic, and dental needs are foldable bags which have a hanger that you can hang in a bathroom or on a doorknob. Many companies make this kind of bag.

37. Soap containers and liquid soap
If you will be camping or using hostels where you need your own soap, use a small plastic soap box or plastic bag to store your soap. Avoid having the wet soap drip over your belongings. Liquid soap is another option.

38. No soap, no problem
Public toilets may not have soap available. Bring a small bottle of hand sanitizer like Purell or a small pack of sanitizing paper towels like baby wipes. These can be gold when you are in places with no running water or soap. You can keep yourself clean and kill bacteria.

39. No toilet paper, big problem
Just as there may be no soap, you may not find toilet paper everywhere. Some public bathrooms charge you for toilet paper. If you have a small packet of tissues like Kleenex, you can use them for toilet paper as well.

40. Moist towelettes
These can be life savers when you are in places with no running water or paper. If you need to clean yourself, these moist little paper towels will do the trick.

41. Quick drying clothing
Packing the bare minimum is definitely advisable in most travel

situations. After you have carried everything but the kitchen sink up and down a few flights of stairs in a rural train station, you will be wishing you had packed a little lighter. Instead of taking multiple sets of basics such as pants, shirts, underwear, and socks, why not reduce some of the bulk in your bag and invest in one or two sets of quick drying travel clothing? Many outdoor and travel outfitters offer highly practical, travel savvy clothing which dries n just a few hours. Wear today, wash tonight, and wear again tomorrow.

Exofficio is one brand offering a wide range of travel clothing starting with basic outfits starting at around $75. Quick drying underwear ranges from $16-18. That figure may sound steep, but considering the overweight baggage fees the airlines are now charging, this investment could save you money in the long run. Exofficio has end-of-season online sales where you can save money on buying their clothing out of season.

www.exofficio.com

42. Laundry soap
Pack a small container of laundry soap so you can hand wash your clothes. If you don't have laundry soap or detergent, use shampoo to wash your clothes. Regular soap can be harsh on colors. Shampoo has milder ingredients that is less likely to harm your clothing.

Guidebooks, Maps, Research

43. Guidebooks for budget travel
The Lonely Planet brand is the most popular budget travel book. However, the Moon Guides, the Bradt Guides, the French Guide Routard, and Rough Guides are quite common as well. Your choice will depend on your style. You can browse through the books and see which ones you like most. It's good to get a guide-

book before you go on your trip so you can do some initial planning. If you are traveling during high season, you should book your accommodations for at least the first days of your trip. (I am not a big planner and I don't map out my entire trip like a military general does a battle plan, but some people like to plan every day of their trips before they travel.)

www.lonelyplanet.com
www.roughguides.com
www.moon.com
www.routard.com
www.bradt-travelguides.com

44. Don't overload on guidebooks!

Unless you are going to a place that is not a common tourist destination, I suggest not overloading yourself with heavy guidebooks! They take up space and are a pain to carry. If you are on a multi-country trip, I suggest photocopying the sections of the guidebook that you need for the places you'll visit. When you've left those cities or regions, you can pass on your photocopies to other travelers, or recycle or throw away the paper. The downside to this strategy is you won't have a guidebook if you decide to change plans during your trip. I've done this many times but it's never been a serious problem. You'll meet other travelers who will let you borrow their books. Many hotels, hostels, and pensions catering to the budget travel crowd have guidebooks for people to read.

Southeast Asia is full of used bookstores for foreigners. You will find photocopied guidebooks and other popular reading material.

45. Mix and Match

You can download sections of the Lonely Planet online, in case you change travel plans at the last minute and decide to modify your route. For a couple of dollars a chapter, go to the "Pick and Mix" section of the Lonely Planet website and pay for just the chapters you need. You download them as PDF files and print them out. You can do this from an Internet cafe abroad.

http://shop.lonelyplanet.com/Primary/
Product/Pick_and_Mix_Chapters

46. Maps

The maps inside of guidebooks are often small and hard to read. It's helpful to get a map of the country or region you are planning on visiting, especially if you plan on taking road trips or leave metropolitan areas. If you are a member of the American Automobile Association (AAA), the AAA offices carry foreign maps. Major bookstore chains carry some foreign maps. Less developed countries may not have good maps available in English or with city names and streets transliterated in Latin script. When I was in Yangshou, China, the best maps of bike and hiking trails were in Russian!

Buy maps online:
www.randmcnally.com
www.maps.com

47. Vocabulary sheet in the other language

It is helpful to know words for directions, food, transportation, costs, greetings, and other essential phrases in the language of the country you are visiting. English is widely spoken in some Western European countries, but not everyone you meet speaks English—or wants to speak English. It's a nice gesture to try to ask for help in the language of the country you are visiting. Usually, guidebooks have a list of essential phrases and words in the foreign language listed in the back of the guidebook. Avoid carrying around a heavy guidebook all day. Photocopy the essential phrases. You can easily fold the papers and place them into your pocket, backpack, purse, or bag for easy access.

48. Guidebooks and maps with phonetic and original spellings

In countries with alphabets other than yours, make sure you get a guidebook, phrase book, and map that have both the phonetic spelling in your alphabet and the spelling in the language of the country where you are traveling. This is crucial if you need to ask for help from locals when you are lost and trying to find something.

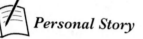 *Personal Story*

When I was visiting my cousin in Tokyo, he lent me a map of his neighborhood that was all in Japanese. He gave me verbal directions in Russian. I got lost. Even though the street signs were transliterated in Romanized script, I couldn't figure out where I was on the Japanese language map. Luckily, my cousin lived near a Shinto temple and I knew the Japanese word for temple and asked people on the street to direct me to the temple. Once I got to the temple, I found my way to my cousin's house without needing the map.

49. Online research

In addition to reading your guidebook, you can do research online about your travel destination. You can even make online acquaintances with people who live in the countries you will visit by searching for groups of interest on MySpace or Facebook. To join the groups and send messages to members, you will need to become members of Facebook and My Space. If you are the planning type and want to decide on your hotels before your trip, you can go to Lonely Planet's Thorn Tree, Trip Advisor, Virtual Tourist, I go U go or any of the other travelers' forums where travelers give advice and rate hotels and restaurants worldwide. Some of the websites listed below have free online guides written by users and local residents for various cities worldwide. (Keep in mind that since the sites are free, they have many advertisements. Make sure to pay attention to what content is user generated and not paid material.)

www.facebook.com
www.myspace.com
www.tripadvisor.com
www.lonelyplanet.com/thorntree
www.travellerspoint.com
www.travelmuse.com (family travel planning)
www.igougo.com
www.bootsnall.com
www.virtualtourist.com
www.globosapiens.com

Section 3: Frequent Flyer Miles

Strategies & Tricks to Get Free Tickets

Frequent Flyer Miles = Free Travel, But No Free Lunch

50. Stay loyal

Frequent flyer mile programs have been my ticket to free travel ever since I started flying on a regular basis. They are the holy grail of frequent travelers, but they are no free lunch. You still have to pay airport taxes. (My "free" October 2008 San Francisco-Frankfurt-Berlin-Frankfurt-San Francisco flight cost around $115 in airport taxes with United Airlines).

The key to accumulating enough frequent flyer miles to earn free trips is to travel on the same airline or partner airlines. Most major airlines work with international partners and schedule co-operated flights. They allow you to accrue miles on one airline when you fly on one of their partner flights. (However, not all flights are eligible for miles. I've had a couple discount flights on international partner airlines that did not count for credit with US carriers.)

I've earned many international and domestic tickets for free with airlines. For me, paying for a plane ticket is a strange concept because I fly so much for free.

Play The Airlines' Games And Travel For Free

51. Plastic = free travel

I accrue so many miles because I play the games offered by the airlines. Each airline has its own credit card that it wants its customers to use. You get a 15,000 or 21,000 mile bonus when you sign up for the credit card. Usually for each dollar you spend on the card, you get one frequent flyer mile. Many times, the annual fee is waived for the first year. Some cards that have no annual fees at all only award you one mile for every $2 spent. With 25,000 frequent flyer miles, you can have a free domestic ticket in the US. If you get a 21,000 mile bonus upon signing up for the card and you take at least at 4000 mile flight, you already have a free ticket.

Airlines say that you can't get bonus miles more than once with their credit card partners. This is not always the case as I've closed cards for which I got many bonus miles and then opened new ones with the same airlines and still got the new bonus miles.

The American Express Gold card lets you accumulate points which you can then use to pay for part of or all of your plane fare.

I have had credit cards from several airlines and have always paid my balance in full each month. I never carry a balance. If you are unable to control your spending and are afraid of running up credit card debt by getting a new card to fund your free travel, then don't get it. I don't want to encourage people to get into debt. We already have a horrible savings rate in the US as it is. Be responsible.

www.americanexpress.com Look for Gold Card information
www.indexcreditcards.com/
http://travel_airlinecreditcards.html
List of airline and travel credit cards with interest rates and mileage credit policies

52. Airline affiliate companies
Besides using airline credit cards, there are other ways to get free miles. Hotels, car rental companies, mobile telephone carriers, banks, loan companies, online retailers, online movie rental companies, and other companies have affiliate agreements with airlines. You can find out more about these offers on the website of the airlines and in their printed frequent flyer mile program brochures. For example, when registering for your hotel, give the hotel your airline's frequent flyer member number. You will get miles credited to your frequent flyer mile account.

53. Airline promotions
Mileage programs send emails and printed materials with their

latest promotions. Certain promotional flight routes will yield you more bonus miles because the airline is trying to get more customers to fly on their new routes.

54. Elite membership

If you fly a lot, it makes sense to stay with one airline. The more loyal a flyer is to a certain airline, the more perks he or she can get. Most airlines have their elite or premium frequent flyer membership levels that give members priority check-in, security and seating privileges, extra mileage bonuses, and upgrades.

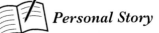 *Personal Story*

After flying more than 25,000 miles with United in 2007, I was promoted to being an Elite Frequent flyer member. This new status allowed me to sit in the Economy Plus with an extra five inches of legroom. I also earned an extra 25% miles on each United flight I flew. I got to move through check-in, security, and boarding faster than regular passengers. The airline gave me free upgrades for 500 mile flights.

55. Don't let your miles fly away before you fly

Frequent flyer miles can expire. Check to see how long the miles will stay in your account. Airlines differ in their policies. Some airlines will consider you an active member and not expire your miles even if you don't fly with them for a while, provided you use their credit card or you register your frequent flyer miles when renting a car, booking a hotel, or with any of their other partners. You need to be vigilant because the airlines DO NOT send you warning notices telling you to use up your miles soon before they expire.

You can get online or printed statements for your mileage balance. JetBlue only has online statements and will not send you your mileage summary by mail.

56. Bonus for online statements

Most airlines will give you a bonus if you sign up for online statements. It saves them money in printing and postage. You can also check your mileage statement online by setting up a password on the airline's website.

57. Flight surveys/contests

United Airlines always sends an email to passengers who booked their flights online after their flight. The email directs the passengers to an optional survey rating United's performance on the flight. Passengers who complete the survey are then entered into a contest to win 100,000 frequent flyer miles. Airlines occasionally operate contests for travel photos and stories to be included in their in-flight magazines. Check their websites or magazines for details.

You have enough miles for you trip. What now?

58. Book ahead

Unless you are planning on going last minute to Siberia in February, last minute travel can be tough to book with frequent flyer miles. This is especially true if you are traveling to a popular destination or in high season (summer months, Thanksgiving-Christmas-New Year, Easter). For popular destinations and times of year, you may have to reserve the tickets six months or a year ahead.

59. Book online

By reserving your frequent flyer ticket on the airline's website, you can avoid the $15-25 service fees the airlines charge for reservations made by phone.

60. Multi-stop tickets

One of the things I love about frequent flyer tickets is that the airlines allow you to make two stops with no extra fees. For example, I flew from San Francisco to Buenos Aires, Argentina in August 2007 for a five day stay and then flew from Buenos Aires to Rio de Janeiro, Brazil for a three week trip and then flew back from Brazil to San Francisco on one ticket. If I had paid for the ticket, I might have had to pay extra for my stop in Brazil. If you are planning a multi-stop trip or will be using partner airlines for your flight, you will have to call the airline's reservation number and make the reservation on the phone and pay the $15-25 phone reservation fee.

61. The website shows there is no availability for the dates you want to travel

This warning does not necessarily mean that you can't use your miles for the trip. Check if you can fly from other airports near your home or near your destination. Play with the dates. Maybe leaving a few days earlier or later will change the availability. Look to see if the airline's partner airlines fly to your destination. If so, then you need to call the frequent flyer reservation number and talk to the reservationist and ask for the person to check with the partner airlines. Changing dates may take patience. You may have to call back several times. If you are flying from San Francisco to Berlin and there are no available seats on flights from San Francisco across the Atlantic, ask the reservation clerk to see if you can fly from San Francisco to Chicago or another big city and then get a flight to any city in Europe and then connect to Berlin. When it's free, you may have several stops along the way, and the airlines may not serve food. Like I said before, there's no free lunch. Some airlines let you hold a reservation for a couple of days as you check to see if there are other flight options and other airlines require that you "ticket" your reservation as soon as you make the booking.

62. Know the change policies

Make sure to ask what the policies are to change the ticket. Some airlines charge nothing if you keep the same itinerary and just change the dates. Others will make you pay to alter the dates. United Airlines has a policy that if even one segment of your itinerary is with a partner airline, you cannot make any changes to your itinerary after you have started your trip. That means that if you fly with United from Boston to Frankfurt and then with Lufthansa from Frankfurt to Prague and you get sick in Prague and need to stay longer, you can't change your ticket. Keep these things in mind when you make your travel plans and remember to buy travel insurance.

 Personal story

I used my United Airlines miles to book a frequent flyer ticket to Lithuania and Russia and flew via United and Lufthansa in September 2005. Sick with tonsillitis, I was hospitalized in my hometown of St. Petersburg, Russia and was afraid I wouldn't get well in time to take my return flight home from Moscow. Luckily, I got healthy in time for my return flight home, but the airline would not let me change my ticket and fly from St. Petersburg. I had to buy a one way plane ticket to Moscow to catch my flight to Frankfurt. If I hadn't made it to Moscow, I would have had to pay for my own return ticket to California.

63. Upgrade from being a sardine to being served salmon on real plates

One of my former coworkers never used his many frequent flyer miles for free flights. He bought inexpensive coach class tickets and used his miles to upgrade to first class. For example, a one-way upgrade from Economy to the next class of service on a United ticket costs 8000 miles for a flight originating in North America destined for North America, Central America, and the Caribbean, or 15,000 miles for international flights. (The next class of service means that if you are booked on a three-class aircraft, you can upgrade from paid United Economy to United Business, or from paid United Business to United First. On a two-class aircraft, you can upgrade from paid United Economy to United First.) If you are on a three-class aircraft originating in North America and you want to go from proletariat seating in Economy to being royalty in First Class, a one-way upgrade will cost you 15,000 miles for North America, Central America, and the Caribbean, and 30,000 miles for most international destinations.

If you buy super cheap fares, you may not be able to upgrade. Check your booking class before you have visions of champagne and reclining seats for your next long flight.

64. Trade points

The Points.com website allows people to trade points between their different hotel and airline point and mileage programs. You can also buy points and miles to add to your accounts and manage all of your loyalty programs on the site. Buying from the online retailers on the site can also earn you points and miles.

www.points.com

65. Compare prices to mileage

If there are special airfare deals or price-wars between carriers, see if you can get a cheap plane ticket rather than using up your free miles. It's best to use frequent flyer miles for tickets to expensive destinations. You might be better off accumulating more miles to use for another trip rather than using them on a low-cost trip that you could afford to buy.

66. Double or triple miles

United Airlines has a program called Award Accelerator where passengers can pay a premium to double or triple the miles earned on a flight. For example, a one-way flight from Washington DC to London Heathrow is a 3,677 mile journey. With the Accelerator Program, you can double your miles for $110 or triple your miles for $221.

www.united.com/traveloptions

Section 4: Transportation

Consolidator Airfare Websites,
Discount Airlines, Airfare Buying
Strategies, Train Passes, Bus Tickets,
Car Rentals

Air Travel

67. Buy plane tickets in advance

I am notorious for being spontaneous. I am also known for not using the return portion of round trip plane tickets. As much as I love to do things at the spur of the moment, advance planning is key to securing inexpensive plane tickets, especially now as plane fares are dear. If you are not tied to traveling on certain precise dates, then you can go onto the airfare search engines below and play around with various dates to see if you can get a cheap fare. These sites compare the flight routes and prices on different airlines. Some of the sites will ask you if your dates are flexible. On Kayak (www.kayak.com), a column on the left shows comparative prices for flights from nearby airports for your departure and arrival cities. You can play with those airport locations to see if you can get a lower price. You can also change the departure times to see if the prices will be more favorable to you.

Consolidator airfares:
www.kayak.com
www.mobissimo.com
www.lessmo.com
www.cheaptickets.com
www.orbitz.com
www.cfares.com

Discount airfare to Europe:
www.1800flyeurope.com

68. Be flexible

Most airfare search sites and airline sites give you the option of seeing fares for your desired route for a few days before and after your desired flight dates. Check to see if leaving a day earlier or later may reduce your fare. Sometimes flying midweek and staying over a weekend can also make your fare cheaper. At times, staying for at least 30 days can decrease your fare. Spend some time playing with your schedule to see if you can save money.

69. Round the world tickets

Are a recent college graduate, have just been laid off from your job, able to take a significant time off work, or retired? If so, there may be no better time to embark on your dream trip around the world. This adventure can be much more accessible, more flexible and even cheaper through so-called 'round the world' or 'RTW' tickets. Instead of booking multiple one-way flights from one destination to another, groups of airlines offer RTW tickets which are valid for a specific duration (usually up to one year) and a certain number of stops (typically no more than 20). Each of the groups has strengths and weaknesses on its routes, depending on where you want to go. Choose your must-see destinations and do a little research before deciding which ticket best suits you. RTW tickets can be booked directly with one of the participating airlines or through a travel agent.

There are also a number of online resources to help you plan your RTW trip. Many of the resource sites are commercial, but are none the less packed full of information such as itinerary planners, sample routes, budgeting advice, blog recommendations, and free newsletters.

RTW Planning Resources:
http://wikitravel.org/en/
Round_the_world_flights
www.bootsnall.com
www.thetravellerslounge.co.uk
www.roundtheworldticket.com

Airline Groups Offering RTW Tickets:
www.staralliance.com
www.oneworld.com/ow/air-travel-options/
round-the-world-fares
http://skyteam.com/EN/benefits/
aroundTheWorld/index.jsp
www.thegreatescapade.com/whatIs.php

70. Track airfares

Using data from past airfare prices, Farecast.com predicts whether a ticket price between two cities for a particular date is expected to decline or increase in price over the next seven days. If the price is expected to increase, Farecast recommends that you buy your ticket now. If it is expected to decrease, the website suggests you wait for a lower price. The technology is based on a University of Washington study and is currently available to search for domestic and international flights from major US and Canadian cities.

www.farecast.com

71. Buy plane tickets online

If you purchase your plane tickets on your airline's website, you often get a 500 or 1000 mile bonus. After spotting a great low fare listed on a discount travel agency like Orbitz or Kayak, go to the airline's website directly and buy the ticket. If you make the ticket purchase on the phone, you often have to pay a $15 or $25 service charge.

72. Bet for a low price

If you like betting, then try your luck with "Name your own price" tickets on Priceline. After seeing the lowest fares on Kayak, Mobisimmo, Orbitz and the other airline comparison charts, you can put in a bid for airfare on Priceline. Try bidding for half the listed price on one of the other websites. If your bid isn't accepted, then you can raise your price. If your bid is accepted, then your credit card is automatically charged and your ticket is non-returnable and non-changeable. Priceline promises that you can save up to 40% on most airfares. You indicate whether you will accept a flight with one or two stopovers and what dates you want to travel. To see what people have paid in the past on Priceline, you can visit BiddingForTravel.com's website, where previous bids are listed for flights, hotels and car rentals.

www.priceline.com
www.biddingfortravel.com

73. Plastic fantastic

The power of plastic is grand when it comes to purchasing tickets on airlines. In most developed countries, people buy tickets with credit cards all the time. This is not always the case when buying tickets in other parts of the world. I've learned on several occasions that not buying a plane ticket with a credit card could have left me stranded. The consumer protection that credit cards offer can protect you in case the airline goes bankrupt, has no working planes, or has other problems. Plastic over cash.

 Personal Story

Oh did I learn my lesson well about avoiding paying cash for a plane ticket.

I decided to move home from Sarajevo, Bosnia, where I was designing economic development programs after the war. I bought a one-way ticket to San Francisco in cash on Swiss Air. It was cheaper to buy the Swiss Air ticket in cash than to buy a plane ticket on another airline with a credit card. My bank card didn't work anymore, and since I hadn't yet been paid at work, I had little cash. My coworker Oscar Sanchez graciously lent me the $400 for my one-way ticket home.

Two days after I bought the plane ticket with Oscar's money, the airline went bankrupt. How can anything Swiss run out of money, I wondered? Switzerland has more assets than most developing countries. My plans were ruined. The airline cancelled its flights. I had a worthless plane ticket. If I had bought the ticket with my credit card,

I would have been able to get a refund via the bank. But, now I had to repay Oscar for a worthless piece of paper. I had already quit my job, told my landlords I was moving out, given away many of my belongings, and packed my clothes. I felt like an idiot. Luckily, a few days later Swiss Air got emergency funding. It resumed flights, but only on some of its routes, canceling the Zurich- San Francisco route. I was supposed to fly to San Francisco, stay at home for a day, and then fly from California to St. Louis for a family reunion. But, with Swiss Air's cancellations, I couldn't get to San Francisco on time to catch my flight to St. Louis. My only option was to fly to Chicago and take a train to St. Louis with all of my belongings. If it were only so easy...

The travel agency that had sold me my defunct ticket had to re-issue a new plane ticket to Chicago, but the day before I was supposed to leave Sarajevo, the travel agency moved to a new location. There were no agents in the new office. The phone in my apartment stopped working. Even though I had already quit my job and my coworkers thought I had left the country, I had to go back to the office to sit at my old desk all day just to be able to use the phone and Internet. People walked by my desk all day long and asked me why I came back. I had to repeatedly explain my bizarre situation with my plane ticket to nowhere. I spent all day trying to track down the travel agents, going to the agency myself, and sending friends to the new location to fetch my ticket. At 5pm, I finally found the agent and got my new ticket. Hallelujah! Though my debacle was nothing compared to the risks people took during the war to escape the besieged city, I was ecstatic that I could at least cross the Atlantic and then make my way home by train, plane— or whatever means of transport.

I flew from Sarajevo to Zurich and spent the night at a Bosnian friend's house. On the next day, I went back to the airport to board my Chicago bound flight. The security scanner at the departure gate detected TNT in my laptop. After being stranded in Sarajevo with an obsolete plane ticket, the last thing I needed was to call my family to tell them I was going to miss the reunion because I was in a Swiss holding cell under suspicion for terrorism, exactly one month after the September 11, 2001 terrorist attacks. More security personnel came by and used a machine that looked like a mini vacuum cleaner to inspect my laptop case. I didn't look like their stereotypical terrorism suspect. The airport staff was really confused and so was I. How could there be explosive material in my old laptop?

"Where are you coming from?" the blond haired, blue-eyed middle aged Swiss security officer asked me with her heavily accented Swiss German English.

"Bosnia," I responded, knowing that my country of departure would raise some suspicion.

"Bosnia?" she asked, her eyebrows raised.

After 15 months in the former Olympic City turned war zone, I had become accustomed to the question. It was just not the right time for me to explain in detail about my humanitarian economic development work, so I gave her a short description.

"Were you working near the land mines or areas with depleted uranium?" asked a young male security officer.

"No," I answered. Is it possible that the depleted uranium in the Bosnian soil could have infected my laptop? I was ready to abandon the laptop and have the security people destroy it. I had to go to St. Louis.

After more questioning and inspection of my laptop, the Zurich Airport security agents allowed me to board the plane with my laptop. I had already delayed the plane and caused passengers to miss connections. My seat was at the back of the plane. As I walked to the rear of the large plane, all of the passengers looked at me, wondering why I made them wait. Luckily, Swiss Air had a liberal alcohol policy on board. Getting out of Bosnia merited a few drinks.

When I arrived in St. Louis, my whole family was dying of laughter from my adventure. We figured that the styrofoam my father had placed in my laptop case to protect my computer had triggered the TNT scare.

Most of this crazy story would have been avoided had I purchased my airplane ticket with a credit card.

74. Discount Airlines

Discount airlines such as Southwest Airlines and JetBlue in the United States and RyanAir in Europe often fly out of small airports, not a metropolitan area's major terminal. Check to see if a smaller airport will meet your needs. Be careful when booking fares. The fares may initially seem incredibly low because they do not include taxes. Also, discount carriers often allow a very minimal amount of luggage, requiring that you pay expensive overweight charges. And often, no free beverage or food service is offered.

Be sure to check the frequent flyer policies of these discount carriers. Unlike regular airlines, some discount carriers only let passengers accrue and use frequent flyer miles within a period of one year.

Intercontinental Discount Flights

Aer Lingus has cheap flights from the UK and Ireland to the US and within Europe, **www.aerlingus.com**

Condor, based in Germany, flies to Europe and the Middle East, the Americas, Africa, and Asia, **www.condor.com**

AirBerlin, based in Germany, flies to Asia, Americas, and Africa and within Europe, **www.airberlin.com**

Flyglobespan flies from Scotland to North America and South Africa and within Europe, **www.flyglobespan.com**

Jetstar is flying in East Asia and Australasia up to Hawaii, **www.jetstar.com**

Point Afrique flies from France to Africa. The site is in French: **www.point-afrique.com**

Zoom Airlines has cheap flights from Canada and a few US cities to the UK and Paris as well as flights from the UK to Bermuda, **www.flyzoom.com**

Atlas Blue has low cost flights between North Africa and many European destinations including France, Spain, Italy and the UK, **www.atlas-blue.com**

Eurofly operates flights between New York and various locations in Italy, **www.euroflyusa.com**

Discount Airfare in Europe

The most popular discount carriers in Europe are:
EasyJet www.easyjet.com
Ryan Air www.ryanair.com
German Wings www.germanwings.com
Air Berlin www.airberlin.com

Check this Wikipedia site for a list of over 60 discount airlines in Europe **http://wikitravel. org/en/Discount_airlines_in_Europe**

Discount Airfare in Asia and Australasia

Air Asia

This is a no-frills airline that serves Australia, Brunei, Cambodia, China, Laos, Indonesia, Malaysia, Myanmar (Burma), Philippines, Singapore, Thailand, and Vietnam. **www.airasia.com**

Tiger Airways (Asia and Australia)

Tiger Airways is a low-cost airline set up jointly by Singapore Airlines and the founders of Ryanair. Services currently operate from Singapore to Australia (Darwin, Perth), China (Guangzhou, Haikou, Macau, Shenzhen), Indonesia (Padang), Philippines (Manila), Singapore, South Korea (Incheon), Thailand (Bangkok, Chiang Mai, Hat Yai, Krabi, Phuket, Udon Thani), Vietnam (Hanoi, Ho Chi Minh City), and India (Chennai, Kochin and Bangalore). **www.tigerairways.com**

For a list of more discount airlines in Asia, go to **http://wikitravel.org/en/Discount_airlines_in_Asia**

Discount Airlines in North America

Southwest Airlines **www.southwest.com**
JetBlue Airlines **www.jetblue.com**
Virgin America **www.virginamerica.com**
AirTran **www.airtran.com**
Frontier Airlines **www.frontierairlines.com**

For a list of more discount carriers in North America, go to **http://wikitravel.org/en/Cheap_airline_travel_in_North_America**

75. Know airport codes

Even though airline reservationists should know world geography, they are sometimes abysmal and may not even know what continent you are talking about. If you look up the airline codes before calling, you can be sure that the reservationist is booking you a ticket to San Jose, Costa Rica and not San Jose, California!

 Personal Story

I called American Airlines to make a frequent flyer reservation to fly to Damascus, Syria. The reservation agent told me that American Airlines didn't fly to Syria. I asked for her to look up partner airlines that flew to the country. She suggested I fly Israel's El Al Airlines. I laughed! Israel and Syria didin't have diplomatic relations and the only Israeli planes that flew to Syria were military fighter jets! I still haven't gone to Syria.

76. Electronic tickets (E-ticket)

When purchasing a plane ticket online, you will automatically get an electronic ticket that you print out. If you are ordering a plane ticket from an airline, ask if you can get an e-ticket. They are easier to change if needed. When you check in at the airport, you can go to the check-in kiosks and scan the bar code of the e-ticket into the machine. (You still have to bring a piece of photo identification to the airport.)

77. Check in online

Instead of waiting in line at the airport, you can check in on the airline's website up to 24 hours before your flight. You can choose your seats and even print out your boarding pass as well as the baggage information for your checked in bags. Bring the luggage and baggage tags to the check in counter when you arrive at the airport. The earlier you reserve your seats, the better. If your flight is sold out or cancelled, those without reserved seats will be the first ones to get moved to another flight. If you hate being stuck in the middle of the five person center seating section, reserve your preferred seats early!

78. Go to London, then hop over the water to the continent

Though I've never done this, several North American and Australian travelers have told me that it's cheaper for them to get an inexpensive flight to London and then get a discount fare to a destination on the European continent than to fly straight to a target city. Several low-cost airlines fly from London to Europe. There are also bus, ferry, and train services to cross from England to Europe.

79. Southeast Asia: Fly to a hub

Bangkok and Singapore are the major airport hubs and there are many low-cost flights within Southeast Asia from both airports.

80. Text message (SMS) updates

When you check in online, you can register for a text message update on your flight status. This way you don't have to call into the airline or go online to see if your flight is delayed or cancelled.

81. Clean cache

After doing a search for airfare, clean the cache files in your Web Browser. The cookies that airlines and discount airfare sites use to remember your data and location preferences may make the sites give you old price information. The prices might have fallen since your last airfare search query, but the website will give you old data. Clean up and possibly save money.

82. Look for discount coupons on EBay

You can find discount coupons for airfare and hotels on EBay and Craigslist. People sell coupons on these sites and then you can use them to get reductions in plane fares, car rentals, and hotels.

Trains

83. When traveling by rail, look into rail passes

Rail passes for are usually much cheaper than buying individual train tickets. If you are already in the country that you wish to travel in and cannot buy a rail pass there, you may consider having a family member or friend buy the train pass for you in your home country and sending it to you via International Express Mail. The postage charges may be expensive but it may still be cheaper to pay for the pass and international postage charges than buying individual train tickets.

Study the rail websites well as you may find some pleasant surprises and important information on how to use the passes. For example, if you get a rail pass for just Switzerland, you will get free entrance to over 400 museums.

Europe

For European travel, there are individual country or multi-country, five-day, one month unlimited, and other types of train passes. There are numerous options.

For example, you can get a German train pass that allows four travel days in one month for $289, or a second class pass for four days of travel in one month in Germany and France for $394, or a first class, 15 day unlimited Eurail pass for 20 Western and Eastern European countries for $796. The Eurail website allows travelers to design their own rail passes by selecting the countries they need. The passes are a great deal. A one-way ticket between Berlin and Munich is $193. For just $96 more, you can travel for three more days in Germany with a rail pass.

Some Eurail passes are also valid for bus and ferry travel. For Eurail passes, you have to purchase them outside of the European countries where the passes are valid. You can buy the Eurail passes online via the Eurail website. If there's an STA Travel Agency nearby, it may be cheaper to buy the passes directly through them instead of paying for the shipping costs from Eurail.

One of the advantages of a Eurail train pass is that you can take an overnight train leaving after 19:00 (7 pm), arrive in a city the next morning, visit the city, and then board another train before 19:00. Those two train trips count for only one day of travel. Make sure to find out how you have to validate the pass. In some countries, you have to go to a ticket agent to officially validate your pass with a stamp. Your pass will come with directions about how to mark the train pass correctly. (When I bought my passes in the US, the directions were in English.) If you make a mistake in marking your pass, show it to someone working for the train company immediately. Sometimes you have to buy a reservation for some trains or pay a supplement for certain high speed trains. Familiarize yourself with the rules of the train pass and the train system as described in the booklet that comes with the pass, or online. For example, in Italy, the word "express" doesn't always mean that the train is direct or fast.

USA/Canada

Amtrak, the United States rail service, and Canadian Rail, sell single country train passes and a North American rail pass that allows for travel in both Canada and the United States. (At the time of writing, The North America Rail Pass was scheduled to be discontinued in October 2008.) Amtrak offers rail passes specifically for California and Florida. The passes are available for national residents and foreigners and can be purchased in Canada and the United States. You can buy the rail passes online, by calling the individual rail companies or via a local re-seller in your country that can issue the train passes. The train passes do not guarantee a seat on any train. You have to call the rail agencies or go to the train station to reserve a seat on the routes you want to take. Both rail companies offer discounts for ISIC holders and seniors. When you order the train pass, you will pick it up at a train station. Canadian Rail offers to mail train passes for those with Canadian and US addresses. Fees may apply. Amtrak will not mail train passes. Remember that the train pass prices are quoted in the national currency. Both the US and Canada use dollars, but Canadian dollars and US dollars have different monetary values.

Japan

In Japan, the rail pass can save you money on traveling on the famous bullet trains between big Japanese cities. It is also valid on local trains and some metropolitan Tokyo routes. The Japanese rail passes are only sold outside of Japan. Consult the Japanese Railways website to find a local distributor.

Australia

Most Austrailian rail passes are only available for those with non-Australian passports. Some can be purchased online or by calling Rail Australia and others are only available for purchase abroad via a travel agent. Consult Rail Australia's website for more details.

International Rail Passes
www.internationalrail.com (This site has information on rail passes all over the world)

Australian Rail Passes: **www.railaustralia.com.au**
Canadian Rail: **www.viarail.ca**. If you are in Canada, you can call toll free at 1 888 842-7245
European Rail: **www.eurail.com**
Japan Rail: **www.japanrail.com** and **www.japanrailpass.net**
US Rail: **www.amtrak.com**, If you are in the US, you can call AMTRAK 24 hours a day at 1 800 872-7245. If you are outside of the United States, call + 1 215 856-7953 during regular business hours (Monday-Friday from 8:30-17:00 Eastern Standard Time, (GMT -5 hours)

84. In-country rail purchases

Inquire if there are locally available train passes or advance purchase deals. Sometimes rail companies offer discounts on specific routes or purchases made a few days or weeks in advance. You can find this out online or if you are already in the country, go to the train station and look at posters and advertisements for special prices.

85. Overnight buses, trains, planes

Sometimes you have no other option than taking an overnight train, plane, or bus to get to your destination. Make sure to have an inflatable travel pillow as described in the packing section. Taking overnight transportation is another way to cut down on accommodation costs. Some buses have reclining seats that make it easier to sleep. In China, there are night buses with bunk beds. The bus company provides sheets, a blanket, and a pillow. Depending on where you are traveling, the trains may have a sleeping car or comfortable reclining seats. The sleeping cars vary from country to country. Many European trains have compartments with four or six bunk beds in a room. In the former Soviet Union, you have to pay the conductor a small fee for the bed linen and morning tea service.

Buses

86. First class, second class, no class

In my many bus travels in Latin America, I've learned that the small price difference in first class and second class buses reflects a HUGE difference in quality. The second class buses may lack heating or air conditioning, a suspension system to absorb shocks, and be dirty. A bus that doesn't absorb the shocks from the road bumps will cause you to feel every vibration and movement of the bus. Forget sleeping pills or a travel pillow; only extremely strong medicine or inebriation will let you sleep. You don't want to have to get drunk on tequila or sangria to make it through the night! The bumpy ride will also bump your stomach until you retch.

Opt for the first class buses when you can afford them. Some may even have movies and reclining seats and a small meal and beverage service.

When you are in the developing world and riding the chicken and goat non-express bus that stops at every town on the road, you may find that the locals bring their animals, produce, and wares to sell at the local market. Just enjoy the experience connecting with local culture. In Latin America, the buses that stop at every village on the road are sometimes jokingly called "La Lechera" (the milk truck), since milk trucks stop to make deliveries in each outpost, village, and town on the road.

87. Clothes for the bus, train, and plane
Always bring a light jacket, sweater, and/or scarf. Air conditioned buses can be extremely cold while outside temperatures are steaming. Airplanes are often chilly, and discount airlines don't always have blankets. You don't want to get a cold while traveling!

88. Go local
Take local transportation as much as possible, especially in expensive countries where taxis and tour buses are pricey. If you are staying for several days or a week, look into the prices of subway and bus day or week passes. Calculate how much you will use public transportation on a daily basis and see if the pass will save you money. For example, one ride on a New York City bus or subway costs $2. A seven-day pass that allows for unlimited rides costs $28. If you ride the bus or subway more than twice a day, the pass will save you money. Passes are also convenient as you don't have to look for the correct change every time you need to buy a bus or subway ticket. Some passes give discounts for museums and other local attractions.

Ask locals which bus routes are the most scenic. Guidebooks often list information about the best bus routes.

89. Private bus companies
Look online, search in your guidebook or ask locals if there are alternate bus companies operating routes to where you want to go. Smaller companies may be cheaper than the major bus companies. In the United States, Greyhound is the main bus company, but some cities may have private or small bus companies operating that don't use the main bus terminals. For example, there are Chinatown Bus companies that have inexpensive and

popular routes from Boston, New York, Washington DC, Baltimore and Philadelphia and stop in the local Chinatowns or Chinese supermarkets of each city and not the Greyhound Bus Terminal. These Chinese bus companies have now expanded to more states on the East Coast, Mid West and West Coast of the US. The Go To Bus website has a list of Chinatown bus services and inexpensive tourist packages that they offer to popular destinations like Yosemite, Las Vegas, Miami and many other places in the US. Megabus is another bus company that operates in the UK, Canada and US and usually stops in major bus terminals.

www.megabus.com
www.greyhound.com
www.chinatown-bus.com
www.2000coach.com
www.gotobus.com

90. Your valuables: here today, gone tonight

Two well-traveled Latin American friends of mine got robbed on overnight buses in Latin America. When you are on a night bus, keep valuables with you and not in your checked baggage that is stored at the bottom of the bus. Bus drivers may have arrangements with local gangs. While you are sleeping, thieves may enter the bus and take away your valuables from the luggage storage compartments or in your backpack stored under your seat. You'll wake up to a nightmare. Keep your camera, expensive items, wallet, passport, and other valuables in your backpack or purse and use them as your pillows so that thieves can't reach them without waking you up. Wear your travel pouch/money belt on you while on overnight buses and trains.

Storage, Carpooling, Bikes

91. Luggage storage

If you are arriving in a city and will only spend the day there before departing for your next destination, check if the airport, bus station, train station or ferry terminal has a left luggage storage area. Many lockers are coin operated and you have to read the instructions carefully to understand how they work. Airports usually have manned storage areas that charge hourly or full day rates. Some luggage storage areas are poorly marked and hard to find. Check the map of the airport or station to see if there is a facility and ask someone who works there to verify if it exists.

92. Rideshare

Fuel prices are high, and your wallet is crying. You need to go somewhere by car and need to split the costs with other people. You want to reduce your carbon output and keep more money in your pocket. Rideshare is the answer.

You can look for people to carpool with on the Internet. Craigslist has free sites in many international cities where you can look for a carpool. If you are planning on driving from New York to Boston and are looking for people to ride with you and share the fuel costs of your trip, then you should post an announcement on the New York City Craigslist page. Go to the "Community" section's "Rideshare" page. If you need a ride, you can also post your need on this page. Of course, anytime you meet with someone on the Internet, you can never be sure of who they are and if they are safe. You need to use your best judgement.

The eRideShare website is also free. The website connects commuters or travelers going to specific destinations. You can post a carpool request or reply to posts from other travelers. Though the website is available for all international destinations, it's mostly used by people in North America with a few exceptions.

www.carpoolworld.com
www.hitchhikers.org
www.craigslist.org
www.erideshare.com

German rideshare (locations listed in German)
www.drive2day.com
www.mitfahrerzentrale.de

United Kingdom
www.mylifts.com
www.nationalcarshare.co.uk

93. Bringing your own bike

You want to ride through the Pyrenees for the Road to Santiago pilgrimage, cycle through Vietnam, or explore another part of the world by bike. If you plan on taking your bicycle on a flight, call the airline in advance to find out what kind of box you need for the bicycle and the maximum size allowed. You may have to pay an extra fee for the bike. Bring locks, a tool kit, bike pump, spare parts, and a helmet with you. Depending on where you will be cycling, you may not find all the items you need to maintain and repair your bike while on the road.

Car Rental

94. Order Online

Just as for airfare and hotels, you can shop online for the best car rental deals. Think about how many passengers you will have and if you need a big car to carry luggage and equipment. Prices vary according to the size and model of the vehicle you request. You may order a compact car and then when you get to the rental agency, the clerk gives you keys to a larger car for the same price. The rental agencies are never sure how many cars of which model and size they will have in stock. If you really do want a compact car for fuel efficiency reasons, tell the clerk that you prefer a smaller car and ask to check again to see if any are available. Bring your credit card, driver's license and insurance with you when you pick up the car.

95. No Credit, more expensive

Car rental companies prefer that customers have a valid credit card as protection against loss, theft, and damage. If you don't have a credit card, the daily rental rate will be more expensive and you may have to give a large deposit. Contact the car rental companies directly to see how to order.

96. Manual or automatic?

If you only drive vehicles with automatic transmission and you visit countries which utilize mostly manual transmission (stick shift), you need to tell the rental agency ahead of time that you need a car with an automatic transmission. Don't expect that it will be available. You don't want to arrive in Rome, ready to drive to the Chianti growing wineries in Tuscany, only to find out that the car rental agency has no automatic cars ready for you.

97. Cheap, not quite

Rental car companies may quote you an inexpensive rate at first, but when you add on the taxes and additional insurance, your daily rental rate may double. Read the bill carefully. If you already own a car, check if your car insurance covers rental cars. You may still have to buy additional insurance even if you have car insurance for your car at home.

98. Young driver

If you are visiting the United States from another country and are under 25 years old, it's best for you to book the rental car from your home country as US rental car agencies usually don't rent to those under 25. For example, Avis Rental Car Company now rents to customers between the ages of 21-24 with a valid credit card and driver's license. At time of rental, they will automatically apply an additional $25-per-day underage surcharge for these drivers. If you are between 18 and 20 and in New York State, you will have to pay a $110 surcharge per day. In that case, you should look for an older travel mate to rent and drive the car.

99. Disappearing rental car

Some times when you walk into a car rental store, they will say that there are no cars available. But if you walk out and make the reservation online, the car is then mysteriously available at the same place.

Section 5: At The Airport

Identification, Airport Theft,
Security Machines

At the Airport

100. No photo, no flight

Just as people don't bring passports for international flights, some people don't think to bring government issued photo identification (drivers' license, state identification card, military identification, and passport) to the airport for domestic flights. Without an ID, you will go nowhere.

101. Roaming eyes, bye bye wallet

Theft in airports is not unheard of.

Make sure to have your travel documents and money in your travel pouch on your waist while checking in at the airport. If you have to take it off when you are going through security screening, put it in your bag so it is not sitting loose in the plastic tray where you put your things do go through the X-ray machine. The person going through the X-ray before you can take your travel pouch from your tray before you get through the X-ray machine.

When you arrive at your destination and exit customs, there may be a sea of people offering you taxi service or to carry your luggage. Among them are pickpockets. Be careful and aware of your surroundings. If you don't need a taxi and know where to go, don't make eye contact and go straight to the exit door.

 Personal Story

A friend had her wallet stolen from her as she was at the check-in counter at the Frankfurt airport. She opened her purse to take out her passport and ticket to give to the airline representative and in those few seconds, someone stole her wallet. The police told her that there was a Latin American mafia lurking in the Frankfurt International Airport international transit zone and stealing wallets from travelers. Since the zone is international territory and not German property, the German police could not arrest the thieves. All they could do was deport them to their home countries.

102. My Flying Passport! Keep your photo ID in your travel pouch or in a safe place and keep copies with you

You keep your passport and plane ticket out when going through security and place them down on a counter to put your shoes back on, then you leave the security area without your ticket or passport. Or, you take them with you in your hand and go to the bathroom, but leave them on top of the toilet paper dispenser. Casual oversights such as these can ruin an entire trip. As soon as you show your documents to the security screener, put them away in your travel pouch on your waist, your purse, backpack, or wherever you feel is safe. Getting to the boarding gate empty handed is not wise.

 Personal Story

After replacing my self-destructive passport that got moist in Kiev in August 1997, my brand new passport decided to go for a new adventure, without asking my permission. I went on a three-week trip to Israel and the Palestinian Territories in November 1998.

I almost didn't leave Israel. After passing through the long security lines at the Tel Aviv airport, I waited for my London bound flight that had been delayed by an hour. When the plane was ready, I boarded the mini bus transporting passengers to the plane. My new passport was in my hand and not in my money belt on my waist. The mini bus made a sudden stop and my passport flew out of my grasp. Yes, it flew away. It dropped into the crease between the bus door and the step by the door. Another passenger tried to get my passport, but he accidentally pushed the passport through the door and it fell onto the tarmac. The bus arrived at the plane. I asked the bus driver for help, and he told me to get off the bus with all the other passengers. I approached the blond British stewardess at the foot of the staircase by the plane.

"My passport flew away on the bus. I can't board the plane. Would

*you please help me find my passport? It's somewhere on the ground be-
tween here and the airport gate," I said, feeling like a complete moron.*

*Looking at me in disbelief, the woman thought that I was crazy. If I
were her, I would have thought the same thing.*

*"How did you make it through security without a passport?" she
asked, not comprehending the notion of a fly-away passport. Knowing that Israeli airport security is notorious for its thoroughness, she
couldn't understand how I could have passed through without the
proper travel documents.*

*She called an airport security officer who came by in a Jeep. The plane
waited for me as the security officer and I drove around in the dark
looking for my passport. Every oil spot on the dark tarmac looked like
it could be my dark blue passport. Luckily, the security officer had a
good sense of humor. He was usually responsible for major security
threats and checking for possible terrorist attacks. My errant passport
must have been a welcome diversion from his regular activities. We
couldn't locate my passport. After 10 minutes, the security officer drove
me back to the plane. He left me with the head of airport security
while he continued to drive around in search of my coveted identity
document.*

*The head of security for British Airways was a middle-aged English-
man who did not believe my story. As we stood by the plane, his staff
listened to me recount what happened—and they laughed. I was truly
stuck. It was the Wednesday night before Thanksgiving so the American Embassy was closed for the holiday. I was stupid enough to have
left the copy of my passport in my suitcase. The security chief lectured
me about always keeping a copy of my passport close to me and not in*

my luggage. I thought about calling my coworkers back in the US who had a copy of my passport on file to ask them to fax it to the airport. The Englishman used his personal mobile phone to call British customs at Heathrow Airport to ask if they would let me into the country. He was afraid that British customs would fine British Airways for letting a passenger without valid travel documents board a UK bound flight. As he was explaining my embarrassing predicament, I could not help but laugh. What else could I do? About 15 minutes later, the security officer in the Jeep returned with my tire-marked passport in hand.

I was relieved.

I walked up the stairs and entered the airplane. To my great disappointment, my seat was in the back row of the plane. As I walked down the aisle, I heard passengers say, "That's the girl whose passport flew away. That's why we are delayed." I might as well have worn a dunce hat and a sign on my head that said, "Yes, I am the idiot who lost her passport on the way from the departure gate." I sat down in my seat and had to take advantage of the airline's liberal alcohol policy. I needed some libations after my tragic-comedic airport fiasco tradition.

103. ID tags

You can buy leather and synthetic luggage identification tags at travel and sporting goods stores. These tags are good to have in case the airline's paper tag gets ruined in transit. It's also wise to put a tag inside your suitcase or in one of the pockets in case the outside tag gets separated from the luggage.

104. Airport stripping

Make sure to wear shoes that you can easily slip off when transiting through US airports, where everyone has to take off their shoes when going through the security X-Ray machines. If you have any metallic objects like jewelry or belts, you will have to take them off and put them in a small bowl that will go through the X-Ray machine. Don't wear clothes with many buttons or anything metallic that may set off the X-Ray alarm or else one of the security agents will have to take you aside and do a manual X-Ray with a handheld X-Ray machine. If you have a pacemaker, metal plates or shrapnel in your body, you need to bring a certificate from your doctor to show to the security personnel for them to do a manual search. If the agents can't figure out what is causing the machine's alarm, you may have to go into a special room and take off your clothes for a strip search.

105. Laptops
Keep your laptop in an easily accessible place so that you can take it out without a hassle in the security line. Some suitcases have laptop storage areas for easy access. There are also rolling laptop cases for extra comfort.

106. Take an empty bottle to the airport
You can't get through airport security in many countries with liquids. Take an empty bottle. After passing through security, fill it with water at the drinking fountain, provided one exists, and have that water for your flight. Sometimes beverage services don't start for 30 to 60 minutes into a flight and you can be quite thirsty by the time the beverage cart rolls your way.

107. Special food requests
In the event that your flight does serve food without an additional cost and you have special dietary or religious restrictions, let the airline know at least one or two days before your flight. There are usually only two choices of food on a flight and you can't be sure that one of them is vegetarian, non-dairy, Muslim, Kosher, diabetic, or fits your special diet. Sometimes the airlines run out of one of the meal choices by the time the flight attendants reach the back of the plane. To be safe, bring some snacks with you in case the airline has not prepared your special meal.

108. Arrive early, be ready to wait

Even if you have an electronic ticket and can use an automatic electronic machine to check in, you may still have to wait in a long line and show the ticket agent your passport and visa if you are traveling internationally. Bring a book or magazine to read while in line. Customs lines can be extremely long.

109. Airport departure taxes

Most developed countries include airport taxes in the price of the ticket. Other countries make you pay the tax at the airport. Make sure to carry cash for these taxes and not get stuck without the funds to pay when you are at the airport. The tax collectors may not accept credit cards. Check guidebooks to be sure of airport taxes. (When you purchase airplane tickets on the Internet, you may not be given this information.)

 Personal story

In Cuba, I stashed away $15 for the airport tax in my suitcase at the beginning of my trip. When I arrived at the Jose Marti International Airport in Havana to board my Mexico bound flight, I checked in my small suitcase and walked toward the departure gate. I arrived at the tax collection booth and looked in my wallet. I didn't have $15. Oh no. My US credit and bank cards were worthless on the island. I was ready to sell my walkman and everything I had on my person to other travelers to get the $15 to leave the country. I did not want to get stuck in Communist Cuba. (My family almost didn't leave the former Soviet Union in 1980 because my parents didn't know that they had to pay a two ruble departure tax. They had sold all their belongings and had no Soviet money to spare. We arrived at the airport in the middle of the night ready to leave the USSR forever only to find out that we couldn't emigrate. Luckily, my uncle was at the airport and "lent" my Dad the two rubles and we boarded our Aeroflot flight to Vienna.) I didn't have any uncles at the Havana Airport and was desperate to find a way out.

In my panic, I recalled that I had hidden the $15 in my suitcase. I walked back to the check-in area, waited in line, and told the airline agent that I needed my suitcase back. He lectured me about never leaving money in my suitcase. Of course, I felt like an idiot. The agent had to manually search through all the suitcases to retrieve mine. I opened the suitcase on the floor by the check-in counter. Relieved, I found my hidden bills. If I hadn't arrived early at the airport, I might not have had time to retrieve my luggage and find my hidden money.

110. Plane delays/cancellations: cell phones/snacks

With airlines canceling flights to save money and weather conditions causing cancellations and delays, the chances that your flight will be changed or eliminated are quite high. When this happens, the lines at customer service counters at airports are very long with angry passengers sitting on their suitcases in despair If you have your mobile phone with you while at the airport, call the airline's customer service number while waiting in line. You might be able to reach a reservationist by phone who can change your ticket in less time than it will take you to get to the change counter.

Always bring snacks and reading material with you in case you are delayed.

111. Call foreign language customer service lines

If you are calling the airline's customer service line on a busy day and you speak Spanish, try calling the Spanish language customer service number for assistance. Sometimes, the foreign language staff are less busy than the English language customer service staff.

112. Check weight scale at airport

Sometimes, the scales used at the check-in counters are not calibrated properly (i.e. not set to zero lb or kg). To avoid being charged for excess weight, check the scale at the counter before your baggage is weighed and make sure it's set at zero.

113. Wear heavy clothing to avoid excess baggage

It is the final leg of your trip and you have picked up one too many souvenirs. Now your luggage is definitely heavier than the airline's weight restriction. If you have already parted with nonessential or unimportant items, lighten your load by wearing all of your heaviest items. Sweaters and jackets can always be stored in overhead bins or used as pillows and blankets. You can also take off your bulky shoes in flight. Books and other weighty items can be stowed in pockets and in your carry-on baggage.

Section 6: Accommodations

Free & Inexpensive Lodging, Hotels,
Hostels, Guesthouses, Hotel &
Hostel Booking Websites

Accommodations

114. Plan for the season

Being the spontaneous person that I am, I don't always reserve a hotel or hostel in advance. In some places like Bangkok's famous backpacker area near Khao San Road or Saigon's Pham Ngu Lao area, many inexpensive hotels and family run pensions are available so you can usually find something without a reservation. However, this is not the case everywhere, especially not in high season. I've learned the hard way that planning can be key in finding low cost accommodations. It's a good idea to book a place for the first day or two of your trip so that you are sure to have a bed to sleep on when you arrive. You can always look for another hotel or hostel once you arrive.

115. Inexpensive hotel accommodation

Hotels.com, Kayak and other travel engine sites can show you low cost options for hotels. Surf these websites and look for the type of inexpensive lodging you hope to find. Sometimes, you can find hotel deals in major tourist locations for $50 to $75 a night. If you are traveling in a group, it can be cheaper to share a hotel room than pay $20 each for a hostel.

Hotel search websites:
www.travelocity.com
www.orbitz.com
www.kayak.com
www.hotels.com
www.hotwire.com

These websites let you search and book various types of budget accommodations including hostels, hotels, and guesthouses/pensions:
www.hostelbookers.com
www.hostelworld.com
www.hostels.com

116. Bet for a room

If you're willing to be adventurous and not determine the exact location of your hotel, you can go on Priceline and state your lowest price and see what hotel Priceline finds for you. The website automatically charges your credit card for this service and you are stuck with the hotel it gives you. If you want to choose your hotel, then you can use Priceline's regular hotel booking option and see hotel locations, amenities, and prices and chose which one you want. Go on the Bidding for Travel website to see what bids other people have paid for rooms on Priceline to get an idea of how low you can bet.

www.priceline.com
www.biddingfortravel.com

117. Track hotel prices

See if the hotel's quoted price is a good deal or not. With data from past hotel rates, Farecast's Rate Key indicates whether or not today's rate for a specific hotel is a bargain. The statistical program compares the individual hotel's current rate to it's past rates. Currently, Farecast's hotel Rate Key works for 30 US locations.

www.farecast.com

118. Negotiate prices

If you arrive by the end of the night and the hotel has empty rooms, you can negotiate the price of the room. The hotel would prefer to discount the price of the room instead of leaving it empty. If you will be staying for several nights or are traveling in a group and will be booking several rooms, ask for a discount.

119. Split a room with other travelers

As you travel, you may meet other budget travelers looking to save money on accommodation. If you feel comfortable with them, ask if they would be willing to share a room with you. This is quite common in the budget travel community.

120. Guesthouses/pensions

Guesthouses or pensions are like inexpensive bed and breakfasts run by families or a small staff. They are usually smaller than hostels and may seem more home like. Some guesthouses will include breakfast in the room price.

121. Hostels

Hostels are budget-oriented accommodation where guests can rent a room or a bunk bed in a dormitory and share a bathroom, lounge, and sometimes a kitchen. Rooms can be mixed or single-sex. Private rooms with one or several beds may also be available. Hostels are generally cheaper than hotels. Some hostels will include breakfast in the room price. There might be an extra charge for towels and bed linen. Many hostels have lockers where you can store your valuables with your own lock. Most hostels have local maps and travel guides, and the front desk staff is usually quite helpful answering travelers' questions.

If you intend to stay for a while, you can inquire about working at the hostel in exchange for a free room. Many hostels employ their long-term residents as desk clerks or housekeeping staff in exchange for accommodation.

An official non-profit organization called Hosteling International (HI) operates hostels around the world. There are also private hostels. Hostels are not just for youth. If you are no longer a bohemian in your early 20s, don't worry. People of various ages stay in the hostels. HI members get discounts at official hostels. Membership rates vary depending on the country where the card is purchased. In the US, youth under the age of 18 can join for free. Adult membership costs $28 and seniors can join for $18.

The downside to staying at hostels is that if you are looking for peace and quiet, you may be in the wrong place. If you snore, you may be the *persona non grata* of the hostel. Loud college students coming into a dorm room after a night of drinking and partying may wake you up unless you are a deep sleeper and are wearing earplugs. Bathrooms are supposed to be cleaned daily. But after several people take showers, the bathroom floors may get a bit slippery. Make sure to bring sandals/slippers to wear in the showers.

You can book hostels at these websites:

The official Hosteling International website:
www.hihostels.com

These websites let you search and book various types of budget accommodations including hostels, hotels, and guesthouses/pensions:
www.hostelbookers.com
www.hostelworld.com
www.hostels.com

The kindness of strangers

Despite the frantic pace of modern life, home hospitality still exists. I've personally housed travelers for short stays. People that I have met during my travels have let me stay in their homes. With the help of the Internet, you can meet people online and arrange to stay at their homes and meet local people who can show you around. Though hosts open their homes for free, it's a nice gesture to bring a small gift from your home country to give to your hosts and their families. (Chocolate is almost always welcome!)

122. Couch Surfing
To "couchsurf" means to surf from couch to couch. Some of us have "couch surfed" even before the Couch Surfing Project was created as a collaborative endeavor run by volunteers who want

to share their goodwill to travelers. The website has over 500,000 users. People sign up to be hosts, lending their couches or beds to travelers. Hosts list their profiles and specify when they can host and the conditions of their home. Those who can't host but can meet travelers to give them advice or show them around, list themselves as available for a drink or coffee. Travelers can browse the listings of the hosts and query people to see if they are available to house them. Travelers also have online profiles explaining their backgrounds, interests, hobbies, profession, and the like. The system works on trust. Both hosts and travelers go through a verification process to determine if they are providing their real names and addresses. As people host and "couchsurf" in the system, their hosts and guests can write them reviews and references. The logic is that if someone is either a bad host or guest and gets bad reviews, he/she will either exit the system or not be frequented by others. Regional Couchsurfing groups get together for social events. When you come home, you can host visitors in you area, orient them, and travel vicariously through the adventures of your guests.

www.couchsurfing.org

123. Global Freeloaders

GlobalFreeloaders.com is an online community, bringing people together to offer free accommodation worldwide. Save money and make new friends while seeing the world from a local's perspective!

www.globalfreeloaders.com

124. Hospitality Club

Hospitality Club members around the world open their doors to travelers by providing them with a free place to stay or showing them around town.

www.hospitalityclub.com

You stay at my home, I stay in yours!

125. Home Exchange International

This site offers both home and hospitality exchanges. If you are willing to exchange your home to stay in another person's home in another city or country, then it's worth checking out Home Exchange International's services. For a $99.95 membership fee, you can post photos of your home on their site and look for potential homes to stay at for your trips. Home exchangers trade use of their homes, condominiums, or apartments when it is convenient for both parties. You can also trade your home for a yacht or RV. Often, home exchangers will include their automobiles as part of the package.

Hospitality exchangers, host each other in their homes at designated times. Your home exchange partners stay with you as guests and then you go and stay with them as their guests.

www.homeexchange.com

126. Craigslist, Vacation Swap

Similar to Home Exchange, you can list your home on the Vacation Swap area on Craigslist's Housing Section for free. Post photos of your home and describe where you live and state which places you'd like to visit. Place an ad in your home city's Craigslist site and on the sites of the cities you'd like to visit.

www.craigslist.org

127. Exchange Our Houses

This European based site is very similar to Home Exchange International. The yearly membership is 45 Euros. The site is available in English, French, and Spanish.

www.exchangeourhouses.com

128. Motel/discount hotel chains

At some point during your travels, you may want a private room for the night. One affordable option are the many motel/discount hotel chains. Super 8 and Motel 6 in the US and Motel One, Ibis, and Etap in Europe offer clean, budget-priced rooms. This type of accommodation may be located outside the city center, so check the address before booking. Otherwise, you could be in for an hour bus ride just to get into town. Rooms tend to have basic furnishings and amenities. In the US, a free, continental breakfast often is included in the price of the room. In Europe, breakfast is available at an additional charge. When looking for this type of accommodation in Latin America, avoid asking for a motel, unless you are looking for a love hotel and want to pay for a room by the hour!

www.motel6.com
www.super8.com
www.ibishotel.com
www.etaphotel.com
www.motelone.de

129. Check the Yellow Pages for small hotels

Travel and accommodation websites may be convenient for travelers, but they are often times too expensive for smaller hotels and motels to advertise in. This can be a missed opportunity when booking your room. These independent hotels usually offer incredibly competitive room rates. Check the local Yellow Pages telephone book or website for hotel and motel listings.

www.yellowpages.com (US)
www.yell.com (UK)
www.yellowpagesworld.com/international.htm
(An international directory of Yellow Pages)

130. Rent apartments with kitchens

One big, money-saving tip is to rent vacation or holiday apartments with kitchens. Using this option, you can save money by splitting the cost of accommodation with other people and cooking your own food. As many of these properties are only available by the week, they are especially ideal if you are traveling in a group or planning on spending a week in the same area.

http://vacation.rentals.com
www.vrbo.com
www.vacationrentals411.com
www.ferienhausmiete.de
(in German, English, French, Polish)

Section 7: Food and Beverages

Meal Planning, Food Safety,
Inexpensive Meal Options

東華門夜市美食坊

摊位号 75   投诉电话

食品名称	单位	单价	食品名称	单价
羊肉串	串	5	饭后	
肥腰子	串	15	火烧	
羊宝	串	20	烤肉	

正宗新疆羊肉串

清 真

Food, beverages

131. Water

In some countries, tap water is not potable; you will either have to boil or treat tap water or buy bottled water. If you opt to buy water, buy a large container of water and refill your smaller water bottles before leaving for the day. You will not only save money, you will use fewer plastic bottles that end up filling landfills if not recycled. Some hotel rooms have tea kettles. You can also use an immersion water heater as described in Tip #14 in Section 2. Boil the water at night, let it cool overnight, and fill your bottles with the clean water in the morning.

 Personal Story

On a recent trip to Germany, I spent 2 Euros for a half-liter water bottle. That's almost $3. Imagine paying that all day long for water, especially in hot summer months! You will use a good portion of your budget just keeping yourself hydrated if you buy small bottles of water all day.

132. Snacks

Buying food at train stations and airports can be expensive. Many times, the prices are outrageous and the quality abysmal. Japanese train and subway stations are an exception as there are many inexpensive bento box meals.

Bring snacks with you. Nuts, crackers, and dried fruits are inexpensive, lightweight, and non-perishable. Yogurt, fruit, cheese, bread, cold cuts (sliced meat) can go bad after a couple of days, so only buy enough for a day or two and re-stock as needed.

133. Mealtimes and portions

If your most important meal of the day is breakfast, then eat a good and filling meal in the morning. You can eat snacks or small portions throughout the day to save money. Many restaurants offer lunch specials that can be quite economical. You may get a soup or salad, main dish, dessert and drink for $10 or less. If you make lunch the main meal of the day, you can have smaller meals throughout the day.

134. Where to buy food
Food vendors near tourist spots are often pricey and not of good quality. Walk a couple blocks away from the Louvre or the Silver Pagoda in Kyoto and you may find some cheaper options.

If you are traveling during the academic year, look for restaurants and food vendors near universities. As they cater to students, prices are reasonable.

Restaurants and cafes frequented by local people are the best bets. However, they may not have a menu in your language. If you don't speak the local language, keep a list of local foods with you that you can refer to when ordering. Most guidebooks have translations and pronunciation guides for the country's popular dishes. Photocopy those pages and keep them with you.

In general, restaurants with multilingual menus are meant for tourists and are overpriced and not of high quality.

135. Go Local
Visit local markets for fruits, vegetables, nuts, and local food vendors.

136. Cook for yourself
If you are staying in a hostel or apartment where you can cook food, you can buy food in grocery stores and prepare your own meals. After traveling for a while and eating restaurant food and snacks, you may get tired of eating meals with mysterious ingredients. Eating a meal you made yourself with recognizable ingredients may give both your mind and stomach a break from the unknown.

137. The food tastes great, but my stomach doesn't like it!
As excited as you may be at the variety of new foods you see,
your digestive system may not be so happy. I love exotic fruits.
Some people stay away from fruits if the local water supply is
contaminated. Diarrhea, food poisoning, stomach aches, and
other digestive problems are uncomfortable enough while at
home, but can ruin a vacation abroad. Spending vacation days
kneeling in front of a toilet to vomit is horrible. Take it easy with
the foreign foods at the beginning of your trip to make sure your
stomach agrees. When you feel more comfortable with the food,
then you can experiment more.

138. Airborne
The people next to you on your flight were coughing and sneez-
ing all the time. The air conditioning was too strong and you
were shivering during your flight. You feel like you are getting a
cold. Bring Airborne or another type of high vitamin-mineral
formula designed to fight colds at their onset. The product was
designed by a teacher who often got sick. The small effervescent
pills dissolve in water and are easy to carry.

www.airbornehealth.com

139. Freezer packs, mini coolers
If you have access to kitchen facilities, you can save some more
money on food by taking a collapsible mini cooler and reusable
gel ice packs with you in your day bag. Freeze the ice packs. They
can keep your lunch/dinner/snacks cold until you are ready to
eat later in the day. You can also freeze a water bottle and use it
as an ice pack.

Section 8: Communication

Internet Access, Cheap Phone Calls,
Mobile Phones, Text Messages

Language Barrier

140. I no speak English. Help!

You need to book a hotel in advance but the receptionist in Japan doesn't speak English or any other language that you can speak. Use Interpreter.com's live interpretation service for $2.99 a minute to connect to a live interpreter 24 hours a day, 365 days a year. Choose from over 170 different languages. Break the language barrier without breaking the bank!

www.interpreter.com

Internet Access

141. Internet Cafes

Internet cafes are usually easy to find in popular tourist areas and in hostels. In the United States, there aren't many Internet cafes because there's free public Internet access in libraries. However, FedEx Office and other print shops offer expensive access to the Internet. Unless you need to use your laptop for business or your writing, don't take your computer. It's heavy and can be stolen. If you have files that you think you may need, save them as attachments to your email account and on a Flash/Memory card. You can use Google Docs to upload attachments and important documents. If you save your files as Microsoft files (Word, Excel), the Internet cafe might not have Microsoft programs installed.

www.google.com/docs

Personal Story

In several Internet cafes in Frankfurt, the Internet cafes used Open

Office software. The spacing and styling in my original Microsoft Word document looked different in the Open Office program.

142. Different keyboards

Keep in mind, if you are traveling in a country with a different language than your own, their computer programs will have menus and options written in their language. The keyboards might look different. Even if they use the Latin alphabet, the letters may be in a different place on the keyboard. It can get really annoying to type on a keyboard where you have to stare at the keyboard all the time to find the right keys. On most PCs, you can change the language settings in the lower right hand corner of the screen. Click the symbol for languages and a language menu will appear. Scroll through the menu until you find your language and select it. If this doesn't work, ask the person working at the Internet cafe to help you change the keyboard settings to the one you are used to. This means the computer will recognize your keystrokes in your language, but the keyboard will stay the same.

Internet cafes geared toward tourists tend to use English language keyboards.

Keep in mind that there are different options for languages that are spoken in various countries, like British and American English and Mexican and European Spanish.

Free and really cheap calls home

143. Skype

With Skype, you can call and send instant messages to other Skype users on the computer for free. Sending text/SMS messages to mobile phones costs between $0.05 to $0.24 per message. Calling landlines costs two cents a minute for most European countries and North America. Other countries cost more. Calling mobile phones is more expensive than landlines. All you need is a computer, a fast Internet connection, and microphone. Most

Internet cafes catering to tourists already have Skype installed on their computers. You can also create a Skype phone number for your area code that will forward to an international mobile or landline.

www.skype.com

144. Yahoo Messenger

If you use Yahoo Chat, you can call other Yahoo chat users for free and send them instant messages. Like Skype, you can call telephones for a few cents a minute.

http://messenger.yahoo.com/features/voice/

145. Buy a calling card and use from any phone

Buy a calling card online and use in 50 countries. Many countries do not have coin operated machines anymore and a prepaid calling card is ideal. Callingcards.com provides local access numbers for the particular cities and countries. First enter the local access number, then your calling card number, and then dial the country code and number of the person you are calling. So, you can call from a hotel phone or private residence and not incur long distance charges because the calls are considered local calls within that country and you will never be blocked for dialing a toll free number. This is particularly convenient when you get free local calls from hotel rooms. For example, the rate from most countries to the US costs 2.7 cents a minute.

www.callingcards.com
www.worldaccessnumbers.com

Mobile phones

146. Can you hear me now? I'm in Tibet!

Global System for Mobile communications (GSM) is the most popular standard for mobile phones in the world. Its omnipresence makes international roaming very common, enabling subscribers to use their phones in many parts of the world. However, not all US mobile phone companies use the GSM standard. Verizon and Sprint use their own system and their phones don't work outside North America.

If you do have a GSM phone, you should check its bandwith, as countries use different GSM frequencies. Make sure your phone will work in the country you are visiting. The All World Cell Phone site has a list of GSM frequencies abroad. I bought a tri-band mobile phone which works with three different frequencies that I used in the Americas, Europe, and Asia. If you need to buy a new phone that will work abroad, you can go to your local mobile phone provider or buy online at My World Phone. However, it might be cheaper to buy a cell phone in the country you are visiting. If there is a second-hand market for cell phones, you may get a good deal. Hopefully, the phone was not stolen only to be resold to unassuming tourists.

http://allworldcellphones.com/
gsm-frequencies-list.htm
www.myworldphone.com

147. Pay high prices for unreliable service

If you have a GSM phone and you want to take it abroad, it may be pricey and unreliable. Using my T-Mobile phone in Germany and France cost me $1 a minute to receive and make phone calls. Other countries can cost up to $5 a minute! Sending and receiving text messages costs $0.35 a message. Unfortunately, text messaging abroad is not reliable.

 *Personal Story*

While in France in January 2008, I sent messages to friends in France to their mobile phones and they never got the messages. Some of my friends in the US received my messages and responded to me, but I didn't get their text messages. In both cases, T-Mobile charged me for my messages whether I received them or not. The T-Mobile representative said that T-Mobile could not control the quality of their foreign partner's satellites. Don't count on sending and receiving text messages on your cell phone abroad.

148. Unlock and go local: Buy a local SIM card for your GSM phone

Call your mobile phone provider BEFORE you leave the country to ask for the unlock code for the phone. Mobile phone companies can take several days to send you the code by email. You need this code for your phone to be able to work with another provider. When you arrive in the new country, buy a local SIM card that will give you a local number. Take out your home SIM card and keep it in a safe place. Put in the new SIM card and enter the unlock code into your phone to enable your new SIM card. You can buy a pre-paid calling card that gives you a certain amount of credit for your phone. For short trips when you need the mobile phone to receive calls and place quick calls to make reservations or get directions, buy the smallest credit available.

149. Local phones

It can be annoying to find out that to make a local call from a pay phone, you need to buy a $5 phone card because there are no coin phones available. Many Western European countries don't have coin phones anymore. It can be really expensive to make local calls from hotel rooms. Calling mobile phones can also be much more expensive than calling landlines. In many countries, the caller pays a higher rate to phone a mobile number and the person with the mobile phone pays nothing to receive calls. Ask the front desk staff what options there are to make local calls. Some restaurants and hotels have small funny looking coin phones that you may be able to use.

150. Multiple email addresses

In the event you travel to a country which has banned the use of your web-based email service, it is wise to have a back up (if not several). In recent years, some regimes have blocked the use of Google, Yahoo, and Hotmail. Consider opening a second or third email account, otherwise you could get stuck without your primary means of communication.

Section 9: Money

Money Exchange, Travelers Cheques,
Bank ATM Cards, Credit Cards,
Fake Money

Money

151. Diversify

Carry more than one type of credit or ATM card as some cards don't work or you may lose one. American Express is not widely accepted worldwide. Make sure you keep copies of your credit card information with you and leave the information with some-one at home. In case your credit card is stolen, you want to know your bank's contact number so you can call them immediately to tell them to cancel your card.

152. Exchanging money

Airport money exchange offices typically offer bad exchange rates. Check the rates in the newspaper or online to find out the current market rates. If you are in an airport and need to change money, change a small amount until you can get to a bank and get a better rate.

http://finance.yahoo.com/currency Yahoo's foreign currency site
www.xe.com World Favorite Currency site

153. Traveler's cheques

A traveler's cheque (also traveller's cheque, travellers cheque, traveler's check, or travelers check) is a preprinted, cheque for a fixed-amount. It is a check issued by a financial institution which functions as cash but is protected against loss or theft. Traveler's checks are useful when traveling, especially in case of overseas travel when not all credit and debit cards are accepted. Banks and American Express offices issue these cheques. They can usually be replaced if lost or stolen and have been popular with people on vacation instead of cash. But Traveler's Cheques can also be inconvenient. I haven't used them in years. Not all banks will accept Traveler's Cheques and the banks often give you a lower exchange rate compared to cash when you use them. If you are on a group tour, you may not have time to go into a bank to change your travelers cheques when the bank is open.

154. Automatic Teller Machines (ATMs)

Most of the major banks in the US operate with the PLUS and STAR international banking networks that allow you to withdraw money abroad. Bank ATMs offer the best exchange rates, but they don't tell you their exchange rate when you use the machines. Your bank may charge you a fee for using their card abroad and the foreign bank may also charge you. (My bank charges $5 per foreign transaction.) If this is the case, take out the maximum you can withdraw at a time to reduce the number of times you have to get money and, thereby, incur fewer charges.

Some ATMs don't take foreign cards. In Japan, few ATMs take foreign cards, with the exception of Citibank. Remember this or you may be stuck somewhere with no money. I had a similar problem in Taiwan.

If your Personal Identification Number (PIN) is more than four digits or has a letter in it, European bank machines may not accept your code. In this case, go to your bank and change your PIN to a code with just four digits.

155. Credit Card Fees

When you make purchases abroad, your credit card may charge you a foreign currency transaction fee of anywhere from 1% to 3%. This can become expensive if you buy many things abroad with your credit card. The Capitol One credit card does not charge this fee.

www.capitalone.com

156. Mental math is not your vacation

If the exchange rate is not an easy number to divide by—for instance, a factor of 13—then round to the nearest number like 12 or 14 to get a good approximation. Or write a little conversion chart which you can keep in your pocket. (For example: 100

units of x currency is equal to 7 units of my currency.) Refer to the chart when you purchase items and don't want to draw math equations in the air. Or carry a small calculator.

157. Coins

It's a good idea to keep some coins in an accessible place so that you can get them easily when you need to pay for transportation or use them in vending machines. It's frustrating to be at a subway token booth without the right coins or bills and have to find change, especially when you can't speak the local language and are in a rush.

158. Keep a stash of cash

It's always wise to keep some cash reserves in case your cards don't work. If you are traveling in the Americas, US dollars are usually the most commonly accepted currency. In Western and Eastern Europe, the Middle East, and Africa, Euros are widely accepted. In Asia, both Euros and US Dollars are fine to keep as reserves.

159. No chip, no use

Some European automatic vending machines require users to use credit cards with small gold colored metallic smart chips or Personal Identification Numbers (PINs).

 Personal Story

In France, if your card doesn't have a chip, you can't use the automatic ticket machines at the train station and have to stand in line for tickets. I found this out when I was in a rush to take a train and had to wait in a long line to buy my ticket.

160. Worthless money

Even if your home country doesn't devalue its currency while you are overseas on vacation, you can still end up with worthless money. Look carefully at the banknotes of the countries you are visiting. Make sure you know what the texture of the bills feel like and what pictures, holograms, and designs are on the money. Merchants exploiting ignorant tourists may pass you fake bills.

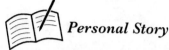 ***Personal Story***

After failing miserably at gambling at the MGM Grand Hotel in Las Vegas, I decided to trade in my remaining chips for cash. The chip/cash machine gave me fake $20 bills. Realizing this only weeks after my trip, I mailed the fake bills back to the hotel and they sent me a check for the value of the fake bills.

While in China, I met tourists who got Korean and Belorussian money instead of Chinese RMB while buying souvenirs in Tiananmen Square! Make sure that you are getting the correct currency before you walk away from the vendor.

161. 100 pesos or $100?

Stores and restaurants catering to tourists may offer prices in their home currency and your currency. They may quote you one price in your currency but give you a bad exchange rate. If this is the case, pay in local currency. If you pay with credit card, check that the charges are for the local currency and not yours. You may be used to signing credit card receipts in US dollars and not notice that your 100 peso ($10) Mexican shirt is being charged as a 100 USD shirt.

162. Paper or plastic?

Ask for cash discounts. Some stores will give discounts if you pay in cash rather than credit card. In Brazil, it's common to give a 10% discount for cash purchases.

163. Tell your credit card company and bank that you're on holiday

Informing bank and credit card companies of international travel is important, especially if you are traveling to lesser developed countries where credit card theft is common and where purchases may be challenged. You may be in a place where it is hard to make an international call to your credit card company or you may need your credit card immediately for emergency purposes. Make these calls before you go.

 Personal Story

I spent a month working in Guadalajara, Mexico and my hotel informed me that my credit card was denied. My sister sent me an email that the credit card company had called my parents' house to inform me that someone had stolen my credit card and was using it in Mexico. Luckily, I called the credit card company in time to resolve the matter and reinstate my card.

Section 10: Health and Safety

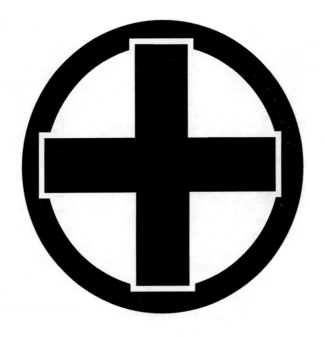

Vaccinations, Diseases, Water Safety,
Necessary Health Items, First-Aid,
Repellent, Eye And Feet Care, Jet Lag

Health and Safety

164. Vaccinations: Get your shots early

Are you traveling in the Tropics or to any underdeveloped country? Are you going in the rainy season? Check the Center for Disease Control's website to see if you need to get vaccinated for any diseases or if you need to take some medicines with you. Plan ahead because if you need multiple shots for different diseases, you will have to take them several weeks apart. Usually, you will get shots in your upper arm. Make sure not to play any contact sports the day of your vaccinations because if you get bumped in your upper arm, it can hurt.

www.cdc.gov/travel The Center for Disease Control's website with information on vaccinations and diseases

 Personal Story

I learned on two occasions that I went to get vaccine dangerously close to my trip. The nurses gave me the immunizations, but warned that the vaccines taken on the same day could have adverse effects to my health. I took the shots in the morning and by the early evening, I collapsed on my bed and was in a deep sleep until the next morning.

165. Take your vaccination certificate with you

Make sure to carry your International Vaccination certificate with you and keep a copy at home. Some countries will deny entrance to the country or parts of the country if you don't have the certificate—or you will be required to get the vaccine on the spot.

 *Personal Story*

After going to the trouble of getting multiple immunization shots to go to the Brazilian Amazon, I accidentally left my Immunization certificate at home. Brazilian authorities only allow immunized tourists to enter the Amazon. I didn't want to get another dose of immunizations in Brazil and had to change my travel plans.

166. Malaria nightmares: Hallucinogenic drugs, nets, and insecticides

Traveling to any tropical and subtropical countries? Welcome to malaria. It's a life-threatening disease carried by mosquitoes in most of sub-Saharan Africa, southern and southeast Asia, Mexico, Haiti, the Dominican Republic, Central and South America, Papua New Guinea, Vanuatu, and the Solomon Islands. Major cities in Asia and South America are nearly malaria free; cities in Africa, India, and Pakistan are not. There is generally less risk of malaria at altitudes above 1500 meters (4500 feet).

There is no malaria vaccine, but there are preventative measures you can take.

If you are going to a malaria region, you can take malaria pills. Be forewarned: some people complain of hallucinatory effects from the pills. Malaria has different strains. If you have left over pills from your last trip, check with a medical professional before taking them for a trip in another part of the world. Follow the medical recommendations carefully. Some malaria pills need to be refrigerated. I took malaria pills once for a trip to Peru and Ecuador and had to take the pills a week before my trip, during my trip, and after I returned home.

In addition to taking preventative pills, you should sleep underneath a treated malaria net and spray yourself with an insecticide.

If you are a frequent blood donor, you may not be able to donate blood if you have taken malaria medicine or have been to malarious areas.

http://infectiousdiseases.about.com/od/novelinfectiousdiseases/p/malaria.htm

www.cdc.gov/malaria/travel/index.htm#protectyourself

167. First-aid kit

Bringing a small first aid kit is important, no matter where you travel. Hotels are notorious for charging high prices for simple medicines like Tylenol and cough syrup. In most drugstores you can buy inexpensive pre-assembled first-aid kits that include Aspirin/Tylenol, Band-Aids, alcohol swabs, cotton swabs, and medicine for stomach problems. If you are traveling to countries with severely different climates and foods than what you are used to, bring Pepto-Bismol and anti-diarrhea medicine. Unless you are traveling to a country with a poor health care system, you don't need to bring a suitcase full of medicine with you as you can buy most simple medicines abroad. You need just enough to last for a few days in case you get sick.

www.adventuremedicalkits.com

Personal Story

While traveling in Chicago in June 2008, I got food poisoning and didn't have my usual first aid kit with me that I bring on international trips. I had to pay one of the bellmen at the hotel to go to the nearest pharmacy at 1am to get me Tylenol and Pepto- Bismol. I realized that the same precautions I take for travel in foreign countries should apply to domestic trips.

168. Water purifier, water treatment pills or drops

If you are going to a rural area with a bad water supply and you know that you may be traveling in an area where you can't buy safe bottled or treated water, you should come prepared with a water purifier pump and/or water treatment pills or drops. Some people hate the taste left by iodine tablets, but tolerating the taste is better than the alternative. You can purchase these items in a sporting goods supply store.

169. Mosquito and insect repellent

Although you may think that any place with lots of mosquitoes and insects would have many brands of repellent for sale, the opposite is true. Many times, the local populations can't afford repellent or their local mosquitoes don't bother them. The annoying flies prey on the exotic skin of foreign visitors. Bring your own supply of repellent. It's also wise to bring after-bite lotion or cream to treat mosquito or insect bites in case you do get them.

170. Bring your own sunblock

It can be hard to find sunblock in some underdeveloped countries or it may be very expensive as the only people who buy it are light-skinned foreigners. You may not even find the kind of sun protection that you need. If you usually buy an SPF 45 sunblock, you might be disappointed to find only SPF 15 bottles at your destination.

171. Contact lens solution

Contact lens solution may be even harder to find than sunblock when abroad. Especially if you wear hard or gas permeable lenses, your selection of contact lens solution may be scarce or non-existent in another country. I paid two times the price of my regular contact lens solution while in a small town in France. Sometimes, you may not find the brand of solution you need and you don't want to experiment with a new brand while abroad. Your eyes may not like the chemical components of the new solution.

172. Medicine

Bring enough of your regular prescription medicine for the duration of your trip and take it on board with you. In case your luggage gets lost in transit, you don't want to be without your medicine. If you are diabetic and have to bring needles with you for your insulin, make sure to have a note from your doctor to show airport security verifying that you have a medical reason to carry syringes on board.

173. Glasses

If you have a spare pair of glasses, bring them with you, even if you only have the ugly pair of Coke bottle glasses that make you look bad. If your glasses break while traveling and you need corrective lenses to see, you might get stuck paying for an eye exam and new lenses. Keep a copy of your eyeglass prescription with you or make sure someone back home has it and can send it to you in case of emergency. It can also be less expensive to get your glasses made abroad. Bringing your prescription can save you money in case you need to get a new pair anyway.

174. Be nice to your feet

You want to walk all along Istanbul's Bosporus or spend hours strolling along the Seine in Paris? Your mind and feet may not agree on what's best for you.

Take breaks. Sit down. When you get to your hotel room at night, lift your feet. Put some pillows or your backpack under your feet as you lie on your bed. It also helps your blood circulation to raise your feet.

Remember to wear comfortable shoes!

If you are in Asia, go for inexpensive foot massages. They can be painful, but they help release the tension from your feet.

 *Personal Story*

While traveling in Turkey, I walked for hours in Istanbul. I came home to Sarajevo, where I was working at the time, with ankle pain. For relief, I went to a physical therapist. She asked me what I had done to cause so much pain and I told her that I walked a lot admiring Istanbul.

"Did you stop, take breaks, and lift your feet?" she asked.

"No," I responded.

"You have to let your feet and legs rest. They hold you up all day," she said.

"But, the Bosporus waterfront was so beautiful," I said.

"You couldn't admire it from a cafe or bench?"

She was right. My zeal to wander and take in the city was detrimental to my tired feet.

175. You'll arrive yesterday (jet lag)

Flying from Asia to North America? You may arrive earlier than you leave because of time difference. Jet lag can hover over you for days until you get used to the local time. If you arrive in the morning, try to stay awake as long as possible and don't take a nap. By taking a nap, your body may go into sleep mode and you may sleep the whole day and be awake all night. Go outside as bright light can help to reset circadian rhythms.

Section 11: Miscellaneous

Unexpected Events, Entertainment,
Refunds, Online Resources,
Bargaining, Etc.

Miscellaneous

176. Budget the unexpected. All your plans may fall apart

Even the best thought out plans can be worthless when something out of your control occurs. Your French train pass may be worth zero Euros when you arrive in the country and the transport workers are on strike and neither you nor anyone else in France can take the train. Your planned vacation on the Riviera may, therefore, only exist in your mind unless you can rent a car, take a bus, find someone to drive you, or hitchhike. In this case, you may find yourself stuck exploring Paris by foot for your entire vacation. If you are going to be immobile anywhere in the world, Paris is a great place to be stranded, but it's a big city to walk. If you hadn't previously packed good walking shoes, you will need to buy some.

Bus and train schedules may just be black ink on paper and not reflect when the buses or trains actually leave or arrive. If you are on a tight schedule and have to arrive somewhere for an appointment or tour, come a day early to be sure of making your appointment on time.

When traveling on a small budget, you will become very aware of how much you are spending on food, accommodation, and transport. Thus, you might not leave a reserve for accidents, but as difficult as it may be, you must include some money for emergencies in your plans.

 Personal Story

My parents were supposed to start a tour of Germany in Frankfurt on May 2nd. They planned to fly in a day early and they were lucky they did. Their flight from Detroit to Frankfurt had to return to Detroit after several hours because of a mechanical malfunction. They made it to Frankfurt a day later than expected and arrived just in time for their tour. If they had come a day late, they would have missed their tour

and would have had to pay their own way to meet the tour in the next city.

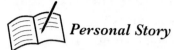 **Personal Story**

Even in organized, industrialized countries, reservations and tickets can be worth less than the paper on which they are printed. A German travel agent booked me a hotel in Berlin and gave me the reservation confirmation. I didn't check the reservation carefully and arrived at the hotel only to find out that the reservation was made for a month later. The hotel was full and I had to pay three times more to stay in another hotel. Because of a big convention, most hotels in Berlin were full.

177. Keep your cool, vent online

The hostel listed in your guidebook is next to a brothel.

The Chinese restaurant in Mexico City turns out to be a local mafia hangout, frightening you.

The tour operator lied to you and instead of being on a five star cruise in the Greek isles, you find yourself on a pre-World War II vessel in a shoebox room.

You asked for a large fish plate and got sardines.

Losing your temper while traveling may just ruin your trip. Life isn't ideal, nor is international travel. Of course you can voice your concerns and complaints to the management of the establishment that did something wrong, but don't expect the "customer service" that you may get at home. Travelers from the US who are used to the "customer is always right" attitude at home are notorious complainers when it comes to traveling in foreign countries. If you are from the US, don't be an ugly American tourist.

Most countries don't have any idea what customer service means. In former communist countries, there were no customers or service, just government run businesses and shops. People had to wait in long lines for everything. There were no refund policies. Even though it may feel like you are visiting Western shopping malls or familiar chains, they don't operate like you may be used to. Don't expect a smile and a refund for your complaints. It may or may not happen. Go with the flow. Your righteousness might ruin your day.

By complaining over and over again to your fellow travel partners, you may ruin their day as well. Make the effort to remedy your problem, but pick your battles. I've seen how one person's bad restaurant experience can spoil an entire day. It's not worth crying over spilled milk or the wrong size fish. It just isn't.

If you want to warn future travelers to stay away from a certain hotel, hostel, tour operator, restaurant, or whatever, you can tell other travelers you meet or post your rants on online travel sites where travelers rate hotels, restaurants, and worldwide destinations and post information, advice, tips and complaints.

www.lonelyplanet.com/thorntree
www.tripadvisor.com
www.travellerspoint.com
www.travelmuse.com (For family travel)
www.igougo.com
www.bootsnall.com
www.virtualtourist.com
www.globosapiens.com

178. Hotel business card

Make sure not to leave your hotel or accommodation without a business card written in the local language. In case you get lost, you can always show the card to a taxi driver, bus driver, policeman or someone else to help guide you back to your hotel.

179. Tour leader's mobile number

If you are on a tour, make sure to note the mobile phone number of your tour leader. In case you get separated from the group, you can call the tour leader for help.

180. Pay attention to directions

When taking a tour, the group leader will give you specific instructions of where to meet after meal or bathroom breaks or at the exits of museums or monuments. Pay close attention to their directions as buildings have multiple entrances and exits. If someone is waiting at the wrong exit, the guide may go crazy running around looking for the lost tour group member and the whole group will have to wait.

181. Beware of cheap tours

Inexpensive tours, especially in developing countries, may be cheap for a reason. The tour guides may make most of their money from commissions from the tourist stores and factories to which they take their tourists. You may spend a quarter of your time in silk and rug factories on your "cheap" tour instead of seeing the sights in Istanbul. Ask how much time is spent on "factory tours". The tour guides will wait until the last customer decides to spend money before getting everyone on the bus. If you are travelling with at least one person who likes to shop, you may spend hours waiting for him or her before going to see the sights.

182. Refunds: Plastic to the rescue

If you booked through a tour agency at home and paid with a credit card, you can challenge the charges when you get home—if you have substantial proof that you were cheated in regard to your original deal.

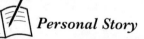 *Personal Story*

In 1997, I was traveling with my family in Peru and Ecuador. We arrived at the Lima airport a few days before Easter to go to Cuzco to see the Macchu Picchu ruins. The airline had no working airplanes.

Customers had been sleeping on the floor of the airport for several days waiting for the airline to fix its airplanes and honor their tickets. The airline could not promise when the next flight would take-off and told us that they thought that we would be able to fly on the next flight. But, they weren't sure. A local mafia person approached us and told us that he could get us tickets to Cuzco on another airline for an extra fee of $100 per person. We had to decide between being stuck waiting for days to fly to Cuzco during the busy Easter weekend, or pay the bribe and leave as planned. We chose to support local corruption and pay the extra "fee." We could have potentially missed seeing the world famous ruins of the lost Inca city. After returning home, we described the issue to the travel agency that had handled the original purchase with the non-functional Peruvian airline and got a refund. The key is to use credit cards when purchasing plane tickets because you can always refute charges with your credit card company. When VISA or Mastercard refute charges with vendors, they have a lot more clout than a single customer.

183. Keep copies of package deals

You booked an all-inclusive tour of Mexico and when you get on your tour bus, you find out that the *baile foclorico* concert and the tequila factory tasting that you paid for are not listed as *incluido* on your tour schedule. Make sure you have a copy of your receipt and show the tour guide what you paid for. The tour guide may be the last person in the chain of command and does not know what your package includes.

184. Pack light, stay light

Venice is your first stop. You buy Murano glass vases for the whole family. You still have three more weeks of traveling and a long shopping list: shoes in Milan, leather goods in Spain, antiques in France, etc. Send the heavy stuff home. Don't carry it with you. Escalators and elevators are not omnipresent. Your back, neck and possibly your travel partners will hate you for carrying heavy objects. Airmail can be expensive for heavy or large items. If you're on a long trip in a country with a dependable postal system and can wait two months, send your packages by sea. It's a nice surprise to get a package a month after you return from a trip. You get to relive your vacation while sorting through the items you sent to yourself.

185. Shop last
You have one month in Southeast Asia and you know you want to buy many handmade silk suits or dresses and other items in Bangkok. Leave your shopping spree for last. If you buy a new wardrobe at the beginning of your journey and send it home, you may have overspent your budget and find yourself broke in the Cambodian jungle with no Western Union nearby.

186. Customs duties
Before stocking up on Russian icons and tea sets, check out the customs fees. You may be buying antiquities that will cost you a fortune in customs fees to export or be illegal to take out of the country. Some countries require export certificates from merchants declaring that the item is not a national treasure or antiquity.

187. Red wine and stinky cheese
Bordeaux, Chianti, Nebbiolo, Barolo... you've bought several bottles of each to take home. You may not be allowed to import more than a couple bottles to your home country. Check on import limits. The great cheese you bought to go with the wine may not be allowed into your country because of agricultural restrictions—for safety. The guard dogs in the airport are not just looking for drugs; they will sniff out your stinky or not so stinky cheese and bark so loud that everyone on your flight will know who the culprit is.

188. Free walking tours
There are free walking tours in London, Edinburgh, Amsterdam, Berlin, Munich, and Paris operated by Sandeman's New Europe.

Tours are always available in English. Some cities have tours in German, Spanish, French, Hebrew, and other languages. The guides work for tips. I took the tours in Munich and Berlin and both guides were extremely knowledgeable about the history of each city. If you are in another city, you can do a search on the Internet to see if there are free tours offered. For example, if you go on Google and type in "San Francisco" and "free walking tours," the first listing is for San Francisco City Guides. Volunteers who love to show their city give these tours of various parts of the city.

www.neweuropetours.eu
www.sfcityguides.org

189. Look for bike tours

Your legs are tired from incessant walking and you don't want to sit on a tour bus. Look for bike tours. Or rent a bike to discover the city. Various cities have regular bike tours. Below are some websites, but check for other cities that may interest you.

For San Francisco area bike rentals and self guided tours: **www.baycitybike.com, www.blazingsaddlessanfrancisco.com**

For Washington DC bike tours: **www.capitalcitybiketours.com, www.bikethesites.com**

For New York City bike tours: **www.toursbybike.com**

Bike the windy city on your own or on a tour: **www.bikechicago.com**

Explore Cold War history in Berlin: **www.fattirebiketoursberlin.com**

Munich, Germany bike tours: **www.radcitybiketours.com**

190. Bring small gifts

It's always wise to carry small trinkets or candies from your country to give to people you meet. You may befriend locals who invite you to their homes or parties, and it is a nice gesture to give them something, even a token present from your country. If you meet children, they will appreciate postcards from your city, chocolate, key chains, etc.

191. Laundry

After telling you to pack light, I should explain how to travel with few clothes. Wash often. Look for coin operated laundry facilities. Major tourist areas, like around the Termini Train Station in Rome, have many laundry facilities. Ask your hostel/hotel about laundry prices. Some places may do it inexpensively. If you have to hand wash, then wash your clothes at night in the sink and then hang them in the bathroom, on the balcony or around the hotel room. There are fabrics like rayon that are especially made for quick drying.

 Personal Story

Don't hang the clothes on a portable radiator. I did that twice and burned my jeans. Both times I made this silly mistake, it was cold and having burnt jeans was not pleasant. I was in Patagonia in Chile and Istanbul, Turkey. Instead of exploring the sites, I had to go shopping to buy new pairs. In Patagonia, I had trouble finding jeans that were not bell-bottoms. I was not interested in wearing 1970s retro fashion!

192. Don't be an ugly tourist

As mentioned in **Section Two**, make sure to have at least one decent outfit in case you visit a holy site, attend a concert or are invited into someone's home. You don't want to be embarrassed or offend the locals by wearing sneakers to the ballet or flip flop sandals to a concert. In some countries, it's customary to remove one's shoes when entering a private home or place of worship. If your socks have holes in the toe area, you don't want to have to worry about turning the socks around backwards so that no one sees your poor socks.

Try not to be the loudest person in a bar. People will associate you with your country and then think that all the people from your country are loud and rude. Be mindful of your presence.

193. Travel partners
If you want to find people with whom to travel, you don't have to count on finding a cool person sitting next to you on the train, you can find them online. Travelers Meet and Lonely Planet's Thorn Tree are websites where you can post where you are going and what kind of traveler you are or you can browse other people's posts to find a suitable travel partner.

www.travelersmeet.com
www.lonelyplanet.com/thorntree

194. Cover your tracks
Despite the cultural richness traveling can bring us, there is environmental degradation left by our carbon footprint. Planes, buses, cars, ships, and other forms of transportation use natural resources and leave emissions that harm our environment. You can buy carbon credits to invest in alternative energy production to offset the carbon you have caused due to your trips.

www.carbonfund.org

195. How many kilos does my suitcase weigh?
It's 40 Degrees. Does that mean it's hot or cold?
Make sure you get used to the measurement scales where you are traveling. Your 2 Euros per kilogram purchase of oranges may give you a lot more oranges than you had expected! Remember

the formulas to convert from your unit of measurement to the new one. Or remember key points like 10 lbs = 4.56 Kilos. You can find conversion charts, formulas and calculator on the Metric Conversions website and convert these popular measurements and others: Celsius-Farenheit, Kilometers-Miles, Kilograms - Pounds, Meters - Feet, Inches - Centimeters, Inches - Feet.

www.metric-conversions.org

196. Free entertainment and cultural events

Many museums have free or reduced admission days weekly or monthly. Go to the museum's website to find out the free days at museums. In the US, some museums have late evenings once a week or month when the museum is open late and is free. Target, the major retailer, sponsors free Target days at museums. You can find these free and reduced admission days on the Community Section on Target's website.

http://sites.target.com/site/en/corporate/page.jsp?contentId=PRD03-002065

197. Mondays and Tuesdays

Many workers hate Mondays because they have to go back to work. Museum staff like Mondays because they can rest. After a busy weekend serving local visitors and tourists, most museums take Mondays off. If you are planning your museum afternoon on a Monday, check to see if the museum is even open. You don't want to miss your favorite Goya painting in Madrid because the Prado Museum was closed. The Mona Lisa at the Louvre Museum in Paris takes Tuesdays off.

198. Free/low cost evening entertainment

Free and inexpensive concerts are often available at cafes, bars, university campuses, lounges, open microphone music bars, and other venues. You may just have to buy a drink or food or pay a small cover charge for entry. Ask in your hotel or hostel for local entertainment that's not geared toward tourists. Meeting locals in a popular cantina, cultural center, piano bar, cafe, or bar will give you the chance to interact with the local community and learn about the culture.

199. "I give you special price"

Bargaining is standard practice in shops and markets in the Middle East, Latin America, Southeast Asia, and other parts of the world. Merchants purposely quote you a super high price because they can tell you are a tourist. They expect locals to bargain with them and reduce the price by 50 to 60%. Don't settle for the first price the merchant gives you. Keep bargaining. For some people this is fun and for others it's a pain. If you hate haggling, then see if someone traveling with you is a good bargainer. Check what other stores have and compare prices before settling. If you are in a big bazaar, you will most likely find the same object or piece of clothing in multiple places and you can compare prices. Be careful that you are not getting fake money in these places. Big markets and bazaars are also notorious for pickpockets. Keep your valuables on your person, not in your pockets. Carry your backpacks or purse in front of you rather than on your back.

If you know a local, ask them to do the bargaining for you as you wait outside of the shop. Agree on your maximum price before the local enters the store so the merchant doesn't see you speaking to the local about the item.

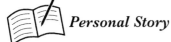 *Personal Story*

When I was traveling in Turkey, some Turkish guys told me that if I spoke in Russian at Istanbul's Grand Bazaar, I would get a lower price than if I spoke in English. The merchants were multilingual

bargainers. There was one caveat: young Russian women in Istanbul were usually prostitutes. Since I wasn't dressed in a short leather mini-skirt and high heeled boots, I didn't worry about appearing as a Russian prostitute and I went ahead and bargained in Russian.

200. Emergencies and consular assistance

There are various reasons why you may need to contact your consulate or embassy.

If you are in a dire emergency, have run out of money and have no one to call or to wire you the funds, you can go to the consulate or embassy of your home country. The consulate or embassy staff may let you use their phones to call home for help.

There are elections happening at home and you want to vote. You have to file your tax return.

You have lost your passport or it has expired. You can apply to get a new or emergency passport.

All the pages in your passport filled with stamps and you need additional pages, go to your home country's embassy or consulate for assistance.

Diplomatic offices usually have emergency 24 hour phone numbers for citizens to call in case of urgency. The consular offices may have limited hours for citizen services. Make sure you check their schedule before going to the consulate or embassy.

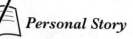 *Personal Story*

While visiting a friend in Guadalajara, Mexico, I decided to go to the US Consulate to get more pages in my passport. The citizen services department of the consulate was so packed with Mexican-American families that the consulate even had a play area with toys for children.

The consulate's downstairs cafeteria was cooking chicken for lunch. While I was waiting for my passport, I had to listen to the loud kids playing and smell the fumes from the cafeteria. It was like being in a Kentucky Fried Chicken with a McDonalds' play area.

201. There's always the Discovery Channel and National Geographic

Despite our desires, sometimes we are just not in a position to travel for health, personal, financial or professional reasons. Even I get tired of traveling. There are always educational documentaries from the Discovery and History Channels and National Geographic. You can still widen your horizons while reading a travel magazine in your armchair or watching a documentary on TV. You don't have to wait in line, fight crowds of tourists and deal with bad weather!

Section 12: Senior Notes

Extra Tips For Seniors

Senior Notes

202. Bring your medicine
Make sure to bring enough medicine to last for your trip as you may have trouble filling your prescriptions abroad.

203. Hearing aid batteries
If you wear a hearing aide, bring extra batteries. Some countries may not have the right size batteries for your hearing aide.

204. Folding seat cane
Weighing about two pounds (one kilogram), the folding seat cane is not just a walking cane, it opens to a comfortable seat that's great for shopping, golfing, parade watching, and sitting anywhere you have to wait in line. It provides stability for walking and a comfortable seat for resting. Costs range from $16 to $30. You can buy this in medical supply and golf stores or online.

205. Compression socks
Varicose veins and swollen feet on the plane can lead to discomfort. Put on compression socks before boarding the flight to keep your feet from swelling.

Section 13: Create Your World Contest Tips and Stories

Extra Tips Written By
Readers Like You

From February to April 2009, Kaleidomundi ran an online contest allowing interested readers to read the draft versions of *Language is Music* and *Travel Happy, Budget Low* online. Readers were encouraged to contribute their best language learning and budget travel tips and stories to the *Create Your World* Books Contest.

Praxis Language, Travel Document Systems, Kaehler World Traveler, Le Travel Store, Calling Cards.com and Adventure Medical Kits sponsored the contest with prizes.

Here, you can read the contest winners' submissions.

Thank you to all those who participated!

Pre-Trip Basics

206. When planning to travel in a foreign country on your own, read about the country with a passion. Study maps of every city you go to so that you know the location of your hotel and places you'll visit. Learn about the shortest and easiest way to get from one place to another.

This allows you to see what you want without wasting time getting lost or going around in circles. If you hire a cab, you can gently make the driver aware that you are familiar with the route. This helps you to avoid being overcharged. Maybe a local bus would be a better choice. You'll know this information if you're a savvy traveler.

I'm not implying that everything you do should be scheduled. Some of the most rewarding experiences come from spontaneous encounters with people, and discoveries of little-known gems not featured in guidebooks. Good planning allows you the extra time for these memorable, unexpected moments.

Anita Goldwasser

Packing

207. Place a set of your clothing in your travel companion's suitcase and one of theirs in yours. If a suitcase is lost, the other person will at least have one set of clothing. In addition, copy your identification (driver's license, passport, airline tickets) and place a copy in your suitcase and in that of your travel companion. Better yet, scan each document and email them to yourself. As long as can gain internet access, you can have those available if the originals are lost.

Connie Gray

Miscellaneous

208. When traveling as a couple, it is best to have the female ask for directions, assistance, hotel info, and any other needs. Most people, both men and women, are more willing to assist a requesting female than a man. A man can be perceived as a potential threat when approaching a female for assistance. Police, who also provide valued information, are much friendlier to women than men. My personal experience with this advice came several years ago, when my wife and I toured for two weeks all over Italy by ourselves in a rental car. Neither of us spoke any Italian. We got lost every day when going into cities to find our hotel. Each day we needed to ask someone for some form of assistance (directions, parking locations, hotels, restaurants). It seemed like we were always lost, but every time my wife approached someone to ask for help as opposed to me asking, she was always pleasantly received and helped. Although getting lost so often was stressful at times, this was one of the most exciting and adventure filled vacations we ever had.

Phil Harris

Personal Story:
What does it mean to be a global citizen?
Anita Goldwasser

My life changed after my sons and I had our first adventure in Mexico.
They wanted to collect insects in the jungle so we left Tijuana by bus
bound for the jungle town of San Blas, Nayarit.

To reach our destination, we traveled on a second class bus with broken
windows. As rain splashed onto my clothing, men with machetes
boarded the bus (They worked at a pineapple plantation). We passed
scenes that reminded me of photos in the National Geographic Maga-
zine showing native women washing clothing in streams. In San Blas,
chickens and mangy dogs wandered in and out of the tiny bus station.
I loved it. This was the "real Mexico."

We made four additional trips, traveling 16,000 miles in Mexico
and Guatemala – immersing ourselves in the life of both countries and
speaking Spanish all the time. What was the result? I quit working in
a lab and became a freelance writer and photographer, selling articles
based on our experiences. My children learned first-hand about life in
both countries and are now bilingual. One son subsequently lived in
Mexico and went to school there for a year.

I was 44 years old when I made the first trip -- and had forgotten
much of my high school Spanish. Luckily, I worked in a food pro-
cessing plant alongside Mexican-Americans and they introduced me
to Mexican Spanish. They chuckled at the Castilian Spanish I had
learned in New York years earlier.

We've traveled on busses with animals as fellow passengers, hitch-hiked in the wilderness, climbed pyramids at archeological sites, and marveled at the genius of the early civilizations in both countries. At Tikal, our small plane barely cleared the trees when it landed in the jungle.

In Oaxaca, my younger son purchased fajas at an Indian market and exchanged addresses with the young girl selling them. They became pen pals. And on another trip to Oaxaca, we sought out her family. One taxi driver refused to take us, claiming that the neighborhood was too dangerous. Another driver took us but couldn't find the house. Finally and old woman tending goats overheard my son and said, "Wait while I tie my goats to a tree and I'll show you where the family lives." She did. I spent the most memorable evening in their humble one-room home, built by the father. We conversed entirely in Spanish. Later the pen pal took us to a church meeting. A 15-year-old boy on my left practiced speaking English with me. On my right, a woman in her native costume nursed her baby. I was thrilled to experience the "Old" and "New" in Mexico simultaneously.

The following year, I stayed at the home of a different pen pal in Mexico City's worst slum. Being able to speak Spanish allowed me to fully experience Mexico and communicate with the people.

My grandchildren now correspond in Spanish with the children of my son's original pen pals. Thus, two generations remain linked.

Bon Voyage!

Growing up in a modest Soviet immigrant family, money was always tight. However, my parents took my sister and I camping every holiday weekend all across California so that we could see the historic California missions and the state and national parks. We started small and then traveled further once we became US citizens and had some more money. When I was 10 years old, I climbed the famous pyramids in Mexico City and Uxmal with my parents. My wanderlust grew out of those family trips and now I am a seasoned world traveler. You can also whet your appetite for worldwide travel with short or inexpensive trips. The world is ours to see and feel.

It's only with travel and communicating that we expand global understanding and peaceful coexistence. I sincerely hope your travels will open up new horizons for you. Let others know that they too can see the world!

May your eyes be rich with the world, your hands relaxed and your mind free from worry!

About the Author

I am a world traveler and polyglot whose goal is to empower people to be confident world travelers and communicators. Via my trajectory through the seven languages I speak (English, Russian, French, Spanish, Italian, Portuguese, and Serbo-Croatian), the nine countries I have lived in, and the 50 nations I have visited, I have become a citizen of the world.

My wanderlust started at an early age, fueling my world travels. While living, studying or working abroad, I traveled extensively in the regions where I was located. These are some highlights of my world trajectory:

Born in the former USSR, I came to the US at the age of three. When I was 15, I was a foreign exchange student in Pornichet, France and returned to France to do an internship in Bordeaux when I was 19. I graduated from the University of California at Berkeley and studied in Budapest, Hungary. After graduation, I worked for the US Department of Commerce assisting Silicon Valley companies to export. While studying Latin American literature and economics in Buenos Aires, Argentina as a Rotary Foundation Ambassadorial Scholar, I interned in the Commercial Section of the US Embassy and worked as a journalist and editor at the English language daily, *The Buenos Aires Herald*. Moving closer to my Eastern European roots, I lived in post-war Bosnia for 15 months designing economic development projects and observed elections in the former USSR. Investigating the links between religion and immigration for a Pew Foundation research project, I lived in Guadalajara, Mexico. The Rotary Foundation sponsored me to do a cultural exchange in Taiwan.

Because of my multilingual skills, coupled with my bulging passport—filled with stamps from exotic places like Tajikistan and Cambodia—some people think I am a spy and that my travels are funded by a espionage agency. Though I was recruited by the CIA upon graduating from university—a job I promptly rejected—I am no Mata Hari or James Bond in disguise. I am a budget globetrotter. With *Travel Happy, Budget Low* you can be one as well.

You can read more about my international discoveries in my upcoming memoir, *One Eyed Princess in Babel: Seeing the world with my ears.*

For more information about Susanna's work, please visit:
www.susansword.com
www.kaleidomundi.com
www.createyourworldbooks.com

Other Titles by Susanna Zaraysky

Language is Music
Over 70 Fun & Easy Tips to Learn Foreign Languages
(Published in Summer 2009)

The master of foreign language acquisition shares her methods to learn languages in a fun and easy way. I have studied ten languages (English, Russian, French, Spanish, Italian, Portuguese, Serbo-Croatian, Hebrew, Arabic, and Hungarian) and speak seven of them. Having never taken expensive intensive language lessons or paid for private tutors, I know how to learn foreign languages in a fun, fast and easy way.

The *Language is Music* book aims to remedy our horrible foreign language learning process. You will realize that you have the power to learn languages very successfully in my fun and engaging way, without having to take expensive classes or leave the country. Learning foreign languages is like learning to play music or sing a song. You don't have to stare all day at verb conjugation charts and get nightmares or fear your language teacher beating you with a stick because of pronunciation mistakes. The tips in this book will enable you to absorb your target language like you would a beautiful piece of music.

By listening to music and the radio and watching TV and films in your target language, you will see that you are learning much faster with this method than from the traditional "memorize and regurgitate" lessons used in schools and universities. The language becomes alive and you are a part of it. You don't have to leave the country or even leave your home.

One-Eyed Princess in Babel: Seeing the World With My Ears
(Published in Fall 2009)

My memoir about how I discovered my global identity via my linguistic trajectory through a modern day Tower of Babel.

At the age of 29, I found out that my world was flat. Unlike 95% of the population, I had been using only one eye at a time and saw in two dimensions. My world turned on its heels. I had always been ashamed of my eyes. In the Soviet Union, I had to go to a day care for retarded children because I was cross-eyed. The discovery about my limited vision led me to unravel a mystery: my gift for languages. I spoke Russian, English, French, Spanish, Italian, Portuguese, and Serbo-Croatian and had studied Hebrew, Hungarian, and Arabic. I never knew why I was so gifted with languages until I realized that my excellent communication skills created the multidimensional world that I couldn't see. Metaphorically speaking, I saw with my ears.

Languages were the lenses through which I saw the world. Each chapter traces how I acted and thought differently in each tongue.

Disoriented by my lack of cultural identity, I lived the life of a global nomad. Via a series of extraordinary events, my Mom broke free from the Iron Curtain by contacting long lost American relatives who helped us escape the repressive Soviet Union. When I came to the U.S. as a child, I faced a dual battle of being labeled "red" and feeling defective for being cross-eyed. Neither American nor Russian culture felt like "home" to me. During my soul-searching quest, I studied many languages and traveled in 50 countries. Whether listening to the melancholic prosody and antagonism of Slavic languages or the whispering and nagging sounds of French or the fun and coquettish charm of Spanish and Italian, my character changed depending on the sounds and rhythm of the language I was utilizing. I was a linguistic chameleon. As a result, I didn't feel attached to any one culture or language, and this lack of identity caused me great anxiety in spite of being one of the few people able to communicate across language borders in my metaphorical Tower of Babel. Overwhelmed with being able to hear and understand many sounds and languages simultaneously, I had trouble finding my own inner voice and knowing who I was. Eventually, I realized that my lack of roots, or multirootedness, actually created my identity. My dysfunctional eyes gave me the ability to be a global citizen.

Illustrations

Title Page: Foreign Money, Sunglasses & Passport

Section 1: Dragon Boat procession, Taiwan

Section 2: Young woman packing younger sister into suitcase

Section 3: Istanbul Grand Bazaar

Section 4: Camel in Cappadoccia, Turkey

Section 5: Airport, Thailand

Section 6: Under a duvet cover

Section 7: Night Market in Beijing, China

Section 8: Monk on a telephone

Section 9: Money Grabber

Section 10: Author with Taiwanese police and Mickey Mouse

Section 11: Calle Hamel, Havana, Cuba

Section 12: Rimma Zaraysky (author's mother), wine tasting in Bordeaux, France

Index

Symbols